For

Thank you for your friendship.

Terry Julian.

IMPROVING CANADA'S DEMOCRACY

Improving Canada's Democracy

TERRY JULIAN

Author of
The Candid Commission
Book Collecting for Everyone
A Capital Controversy
A British Lion
Be Amusing

Published by Signature Publishing
in co-operation with Trafford Publishing
2002

© Copyright 2002 Terry Julian. All rights reserved.

No part of this book may be reproduced by any means without the prior written permission of the publisher, with the exception of brief passages in reviews. Any request for photocopying or other reprographic copying of any part of this book must be directed in writing to the Canadian Copyright Licensing Agency.

Printed in Victoria, Canada

National Library of Canada Cataloguing in Publication Data

```
Julian, Terry, 1922-
   Improving Canada's democracy
   Includes bibliographical references.
   ISBN 1-55212-877-6
   1. Canada--Politics and government.
   2. Democracy--Canada.   I. Title.
JL15.J84 2001          320.471           C2001-910820-6
```

TRAFFORD

This book was published *on-demand* **in cooperation with Trafford Publishing.**
On-demand publishing is a unique process and service of making a book available for retail sale to the public taking advantage of on-demand manufacturing and Internet marketing.
On-demand publishing includes promotions, retail sales, manufacturing, order fulfilment, accounting and collecting royalties on behalf of the author.

Suite 6E, 2333 Government St., Victoria, B.C. V8T 4P4, CANADA
Phone   250-383-6864   Toll-free   1-888-232-4444 (Canada & US)
Fax   250-383-6804   E-mail   sales@trafford.com
Web site www.trafford.com   TRAFFORD PUBLISHING IS A DIVISION OF TRAFFORD HOLDINGS LTD.
Trafford Catalogue #01-0279   www.trafford.com/robots/01-0279.html

10   9   8   7   6   5   4   3

For future generations of Canadians with the hope that they will live in a more democratic Canada which is theirs by right of inheritance.

Contents

CHAPTER ONE
Our Democratic Responsibility / 9

CHAPTER TWO
Our Vote / 18

CHAPTER THREE
Our Referendums / 36

CHAPTER FOUR
Our Senate / 41

CHAPTER FIVE
Amending Our Constitution / 47

CHAPTER SIX
Our Patronage / 60

CHAPTER SEVEN
Our News Media and
Our Political Polls / 65

CHAPTER EIGHT
Our House of Commons, Our Legislatures
and Our Political Parties / 89

CHAPTER NINE
Our Democratic Future / 98

References / 101

Index / 106

CHAPTER ONE
Our Democratic Responsibility

"Ignorance is an evil weed, which dictators may cultivate among their dupes, but which no democracy can afford among its citizens."
—William Beveridge, (1879-1963), British economist

Democracy has its roots in the Greek word *demokratia* meaning people power. It is on behalf of the people that power is used. The citizens have their power to freely choose their government and it exists to serve its citizens.

Canada is one of the freest, fairest and finest countries in the world. How can we keep that reputation and, indeed, improve upon it? The thesis of this book is that Canadian democracy can be made better.

The challenge is to upgrade our democracy so that citizens will want to participate and so that our municipal, provincial and federal politicians, by their skill, credibility and integrity, will be more visionary and work harder to deserve our loyalty and respect.

The slender power base of the Canadian citizen must be strengthened by more democratic participation. This must occur in spite of the fact that the Canadian political system is well respected internationally and serves as a model for many other countries of the world.

Certainly, there are problems associated with Canadian democracy. Most Canadians no longer think that volunteer political activity is an important contribution to their community, province or country. Even though they believe that municipal, provincial and federal government is relevant, they do not seem to believe that politics is relevant. But citizenship must always be active rather than passive and politics should be the part-time profession of every citizen.

Canada is not in crisis or disintegration despite the threat of Quebec separatism and in spite of writers like Joe Armstrong who says that, "Canada is a nation in name only." Or Barbara Yaffe of the *Vancouver Sun* who writes, "It can be fairly stated that Canada is now the closest thing to a dictatorship that a country can be while still being democratic."

Personal freedom exists in the mind of each citizen devoted to preserving it. And an individual is the most important unit. Each of us is unique and special and has a responsibility to work to improve Canadian democracy. Citizenship is about obligation.

Next in importance is the family, in which parents should make themselves necessary to their children and to each other. What is good for families is good for the nation!

A larger unit is the neighbourhood or community, then the village or city. Still greater is the region or province and finally our nation Canada.

Rapid changes in our economy and our culture have created a strong reaction in Canada which includes a belief that all levels of government are not truly democratic and are inaccessible to the average citizen. Far too many Canadians are political heathens who do not participate, rather than political believers who are involved. It is estimated that only four or five percent of the electorate involve themselves continuously in political parties at the federal and provincial levels. Unfortunately, too, many Canadians feel they have far more sense of effective connection within an advocacy, interest, or protest group like the Council of Canadians or the National Citizens Coalition than within a political party. These interest groups promote a rainbow of causes which cross all constituency boundaries but do little to help democracy. As John Saul, husband of Governor-General Adrienne Clarkson, said in the *Vancouver Sun* on April 20, 2001, "Reform tends to come when reformers join the democratic process. A cause really only makes ethical, utilitarian and social sense when it and its proponents are integrated into the democratic system."

In a democracy the liberty of citizens is an end in itself. Statesmen don't think of it as an annoyance. On the contrary they want it and encourage it as the surest guide to the common good. Democracy is not a perfect form of government. What holds us to it is not that it is faultless but that it is less faulty than any other system.

One very important democratic problem will only be cursorily examined in this book—the possible secession of Quebec. This is an extremely complicated matter. Proposals range from Serge Loyal, Liberal senator from Quebec, stating that no province has the right to secede and that there can be no secession on demand, to former Premier Bouchard's remarks on Quebec's right to frame the question and break away on a "yes" vote of 50 percent plus one.

Naturally there are difficulties in a country with two official languages but multicultural education must not be allowed to produce cultural disunity. Education in English and in French should be concerned with making everyone in Canada Canadian.

What would it mean if Quebec separated?

There is a story in which a Canadian aboriginal leader was trying to convince tribal chiefs to join together. He took a stick and broke it. Then he secured a number of sticks and had each chief attempt to break the bundle which of course they could not do.

If Quebec with its energetic, decent and tolerant people separated, Canada would be weaker because Quebec is one of the larger indispensable elements in our Canadian cluster. It would mean that this nation, as one of the most generous, peaceful and democratic in the world, would be prevented from showing vital leadership and from acting as a model for other countries to emulate. Canada, today, is a humanitarian land which has the potential to alleviate and prevent suffering from poverty, famine and, yes, even warfare in other countries. With Quebec, we represent a democratic system of values which can profoundly influence civilization in this millennium. Francophones with their civility, gentility, religious faith, distinct culture and democratic ideals will help to provide a thrust which cannot be measured but will be vital for Canada's future role in the world.

When we look at Canadian political history since Confederation we see the tremendous leadership contribution that our francophone prime ministers have given to our country. Sir Wilfred Laurier, Louis St. Laurent, Pierre Trudeau and Jean Chretien have been and are a significant part of that effectiveness. All of the above have tried to be forces of unity as opposed to the forces of division. This important leadership from Quebec would not continue if Quebec separated.

Deep patriotic feelings and pride in Canada would also be depleted. Some of us remember the joyous and thankful celebrations of 1967 which were a salute to our land and our people for what was accomplished in the first century of Confederation. Older Canadian adults will recall the Confederation train and the trailer-truck caravans which visited 700 sites in all the provinces and territories. Over 2000 projects, mostly involving construction of cultural and recreational buildings, blossomed across the whole country. At that time there was a coming together of Canadians in common pride and there was also a determination to make Canada greater and more united with the friendly understanding of all citizens. This despite our people being divided by great distances and by language. If Quebec left how could we dedicate ourselves to the task of making the second century of Confederation as good, as fruitful and as admirable as the first?

The Olympic Games gives another reason to be proud of Canada. We cheer francophone participation each time just as we cheer anglophone involvement. That pride would be reduced if Quebec separated.

The failure of our nation to accommodate our French-speaking minority would also have a fateful significance. Canada was built on respect for people of all nationalities and each has added to our identity. Confederation has provided a democratic means of achieving co-existence for all within a constitutional framework. It has assisted in harmonizing cultural diversities in a truly unique Canadian way.

As the aboriginal chief showed, there is strength in unity. If Quebec departed it would mean a disintegration of our national treasure—our country Canada. Ethnicity is not as important as patriotism. Canadian multiculturalism is a beacon for the rest of the world.

The unique character of Quebec and the equality of the provinces can be reconciled if we admit that equality is not the same as uniformity. We must show that different populations can live in harmony within a single state. As Pierre Elliott Trudeau said in 1968, "Of course, a bilingual state is more expensive than a unilingual one, but it is a richer state." It is estimated that today there are about 3000 human groups who are conscious of a collective identity. Imagine the nightmare of that many more independent countries in our world. The sentiments expressed by the author regarding opposition to Quebec separation apply equally to British Columbia and Alberta.

On a long-term basis, democracy in Canada will improve when the curriculum of our schools reflects the importance of participation in political life. Teachers must understand and teach how fundamental democracy is in our lives. History may be taught in the traditional manner of dates, explorers, wars and settlers but must also be directed in those facets to show the gradual growth of democracy for every citizen.

The publication of Jack Granatstein's *Who Killed Canadian History?* in 1998 has served to crystallize a variety of diverse concerns about the teaching of history in Canada. Granatstein cited recent surveys that showed many Canadians did not know even the most basic facts of Canadian history and that history had lost its traditional place in school curricula. He went on to argue that historians had lost touch with the public and were so preoccupied with diversity and difference that they no longer told the national story. To correct this state of affairs, he called for a return to national history, organized around a narrative of political development and embodied in a set of national standards.

Joe Clark, in his book *A Nation Too Good to Lose*, reinforces the concept of the importance of history.

"If we are serious about keeping and building a large Canada, we must encourage more schools to teach more facts about the history and nature of our country. It should not be propaganda, because that is not who we are. But it should tell the Canadian story honestly, and reasonably fully, and in the same way in every part of Canada. That will help young Canadians know what they are part of, and prepare them better, if the time comes, to judge whether the Canadian community is worth keeping."

Judgement is an essential purpose of education and an understanding of history should be a vital ingredient in that process for all students. Our schools must not only promote good citizenship but stress the vital importance of involvement in democracy. Lip service and vague generalizations are no longer good enough. There is nothing wrong with teachers stating that each one of us should join a political party of choice. It means a renaissance of commitment which must be fostered in our schools.

For many secondary schools the existence of a student council is the only effort to promote democracy. Teachers at all levels should help students understand about fair and ethical democratic elections—no name calling, no destruction of election signs, no discrimination of groups, no vandalism, etc.

It is the author's hope that all high school students should have an opportunity for a sponsored field trip to their provincial legislature and a trip to Ottawa with a tour of their parliament buildings. The provinces would have to be significant participants in a process of this magnitude.

Other historical places that could be visited by students include Laurier House where Sir Wilfred Laurier lived for 22 years and where William Lyon Mackenzie King lived for 27, the National War Memorial, the Supreme Court of Canada building, the National Library, the Prime Minister's residence at 24 Sussex Drive and Rideau Hall, the governor-general's home.

It was offensive to this author to learn that the Victorian home on the Ottawa River (Earnscliff) that Sir John A. Macdonald lived in from 1871 until his death in 1891 is the residence of the British High Commissioner as it was purchased in 1930 by the British government. Our Canadian government should take steps immediately to acquire Earnscliffe and hold it in perpetuity as a national historic shrine for the Canadian people.

Good citizenship does not happen naturally, particularly with young people. If the following legislation was passed by the House of Commons, it would be a start in the direction of more pride in Canada.

Canadian Flag for Grade Classrooms

Whereas our great country Canada is in danger of being divided, and

Whereas our hope for a permanently united Canada depends to a large degree on our young Canadians, and

Whereas patriotic loyalty to Canada must supersede patriotic loyalty to the province,

OUR DEMOCRATIC RESPONSIBILITY

Therefore, be it resolved that Parliament provide, at no cost to the province and at the request of the province, a Canadian flag for every classroom from kindergarten to grade twelve in that province.

Students at all levels must be taught to realize that a vote is a basic value in our democratic system and the next chapter will show how this prerogative may become more effective.

It is clear that education should not continue business as usual because many Canadians are becoming skeptical of political vision, political goals, a political sense of purpose, and political participation. It will require a "permanent revolution" in teaching history.

Most political parties have few policies to promote better Canadian democracy. Efforts to increase participatory democracy and responsibility in the country must be the commitment of all of us.

CHAPTER TWO
Our Vote

"We must ensure that every region, every province and territory, every community, and every citizen has a strong voice and can contribute to building our nation."
—Governor-General Adrienne Clarkson
(throne speech)

A citizen's right to vote in free elections is the most important fundamental freedom a Canadian has. How may citizens use that vote wisely? Obviously, by becoming informed about political parties, platforms, candidates and issues. The best way to become knowledgeable is by joining a political party. And the more people who become card-carrying members of a party the better Canadian democracy will be.

Why? Because additional persons participating in a political party means a greater selection of candidates at provincial and federal levels. Inevitably, larger constituency organizations will produce better candidates in all parties and qualified candidates means that the person elected will be ultimately more outstanding. Thus, our provincial legislature and our federal parliament will be composed of a more effective group of people than we now have.

Then, too, any political riding organization with many

members would be more active. Policies would be increasingly debated, voting for delegates to policy conventions would be competitive, and contests for the election of the executive officers would result in more competent persons selected.

The ultimate goal of all this is to improve the motivation, skills, abilities and dedication of all candidates for an election, be it municipal, provincial or federal.

Because democracy is hard work involving political duties and responsibilities as well as rights, most Canadians have relatively weak long-term attachments to parties and a stronger responsiveness to leaders, issues, or political events like elections. The federal electoral process is a short-term happening of thirty-six days and citizens react to events as they unfold rather than to the ideologies of parties. Less than a third of Canadians decide their voting choice well in advance of an election. The other two-thirds of all voters will decide during the course of the election itself. For these persons Canadian politics have become a show at election time where television, opinion polls, negative advertising, media hype and phone banks are organized by paid professionals who market parties and candidates as though they were selling beer or running shoes.

This is one more reason why many Canadians simply don't vote. In the 1997 federal election, 33 percent of eligible voters did not exercise their franchise. This was the highest number of non-voters since 1900, exceeded only by the 2000 federal election when only 60.5 percent voted. The election 2000 dismal participation rate gives Canada one of the worst records among the twenty-nine industrialized countries in the Organization for Economic

Cooperation and Development, ahead only of Poland, Switzerland and the United States. (In the latter country voters must register beforehand to be eligible to vote—an average of 53 percent vote.)

Voter Turnout at Canadian Federal Elections and Referendums (1900-2000)

Date of election/ referendum	Population	Electors on Lists	Total ballots cast	Voter Turnout (%)
7 November 1900	4,833,000	1,167,402	958,497	77.4
2 November 1904	5,371,000	1,385,440	1,036,878	71.6
26 October 1908	5,371,000	1,463,591	1,180,820	70.3
21 September 1911	7,204,527	1,820,742	1,314,953	70.2
17 December 1917	7,591,971	2,093,799	1,892,741	75.0
6 December 1921	8,706,211	4,435,310	3,139,306	67.7
29 October 1925	8,776,352	4,608,636	3,168,412	66.4
14 September 1926	8,887,952	4,665,381	3,273,062	67.7
28 July 1930	8,887,952	5,135,971	3,922,481	73.5
14 October 1935	10,367,063	5,918,207	4,452,675	74.2
26 March 1940	10,429,169	6,588,888	4,672,531	69.9
27 April 1942 (referendum)	11,494,627	6,502,234	4,638,847	71.3
11 June 1945	11,494,627	6,952,445	5,305,193	75.3
27 June 1949	11,823,649	7,893,629	5,903,572	73.8
10 August 1953	14,003,704	8,401,691	5,701,963	67.5
10 June 1957	16,073,970	8,902,125	6,680,690	74.1
31 March 1958	16,073,970	9,131,200	7,357,139	79.4
18 June 1962	18,238,247	9,700,325	7,772,656	79.0
8 April 1963	18,238,247	9,910,757	7,958,636	79.2
8 November 1965	18,238,247	10,274,904	7,796,728	74.8
25 June 1968	20,014,880	10,860,888	8,217,916	75.7
30 October 1972	21,568,311	13,000,778	9,974,661	76.7
8 July 1974	21,568,311	13,620,353	9,671,002	71.0
22 May 1979	22,992,604	15,233,653	11,541,000	75.7
18 February 1980	22,992,604	15,890,416	11,015,514	69.3
4 September 1984	24,343,181	16,774,941	12,638,424	75.3
21 November 1988	25,309,331	17,639,001	13,281,191	75.3
26 October 1992 (referendum)	20,400,896	13,725,966	9,855,978	71.8
25 October 1993	27,296,859	19,906,796	13,863,135	69.6
2 June 1997	28,846,761	19,662,522	13,171,628	67.0
27 November 2000	31,000,000	21,161,565	12,804,940	60.5

Report of the Chief Electoral officer from "A History of the Vote in Canada"

Canada's chief electoral officer, Jean-Pierre Kingsley, said, after the 2000 election, that mandatory voting in federal elections as is done in Australia and other countries, may be necessary to preserve democracy in Canada.

This author strongly opposes mandatory voting and proposes that the percentage will go up if the suggestions in this book for the improvement of Canada's democracy are followed. However, it should be noted that in Australia one can choose not to vote as long as he or she appears at the polling place in order to cross one's name off the electoral list. The small fine imposed on those who do not turn up on election day (or who do not send in a postal vote) is not a criminal offense.

A further breakdown (see table on following page) shows the percentage of voter turnout at Federal Elections and Referendums by Province and Territory.

To have a better democracy, political parties must have the support of the majority of Canadians. Low voter turnouts begin to erode democracy and lead to the election of governments that are out of touch with the citizens. In the table, Quebec dropped from 73.2 percent in 1997 to 64.1 percent in 2000. Ontario had 58.1 percent from 66. The last election for the president of the United States indicated the importance of every vote.

Some blame for voting apathy can be laid on the media which has the task of informing the voting public. But even if this is done well, the number of information outlets presents a bewildering choice for a person who wants to be an informed voter and who does not belong to a political party.

There are two further problems in Canada in connection with your vote: voting inequality and unequal provincial representation in the House of Commons.

Percentage of voter turnout at Federal Elections and Referendums by Province and Territory

Date of election/referendum	Nfld.	P.E.I.	N.S.	N.B.	Que.	Ont.	Man.	Sask.	Alta.	B.C.	N.W.T.	Yukon	Canada
7 November 1900		∶	77	73	70	70	65	∶		69	76		77
3 November 1904		∶	73	77	70	77	69			56	72		72
26 October 1908		∶	73	78	69	68	81			54		87	70
21 September 1911		∶	83	78	71	69	79	63	65	53		83	70
17 December 1917		76	80	89	76	79	79	70	76	83		56	75
6 December 1921		79	69	64	75	63	65	67	63	67		83	68
29 October 1925		76	70	61	72	65	68	57	57	75		78	67
14 September 1926		84	72	68	71	64	77	70	57	71		80	68
28 July 1930		89	83	78	76	69	72	81	66	73		82	73
14 October 1935		80	76	77	74	74	75	77	65	76		82	70
26 March 1940		78	70	68	66	69	74	77	63	76		82	70
27 April 1942*		57	45	63	76	64	67	59	65	69	62	58	71
11 June 1945		81	72	78	73	75	76	85	73	80	63	75	
27 June 1949	58	85	75	79	74	75	72	79	69	69		76	74
10 August 1953	57	83	72	78	69	67	59	74	63	65	63	76	67
10 June 1957	52	85	81	81	72	74	74	81	73	74	63	89	74
xx March 1958	79	88	84	85	79	79	80	82	74	76	74	90	79
18 June 1962	72	90	84	83	78	80	77	85	74	78	72	88	79
8 April 1963	69	84	82	81	76	81	78	83	79	80	73	88	79
8 November 1965	66	88	82	80	71	77	74	80	74	75	76	86	75
25 June 1968	68	88	82	80	72	77	76	81	73	76	69	87	76
30 October 1972	63	86	80	77	76	77	74	79	76	73	73	79	77
8 July 1974	57	80	74	71	67	74	70	72	67	72	61	67	71
22 May 1979	60	81	75	74	76	78	77	79	68	75	70	74	76
18 February 1980	59	79	72	71	68	72	69	71	61	71	67	69	69
4 September 1984	65	85	75	77	76	76	73	78	69	78	68	78	75
21 November 1988	67	85	75	76	75	75	75	78	75	79	71	78	75
26 October 1992*	53	71	68	72	70	72	71	69	73	77	70	70	72
25 October 1993	55	73	64	69	77	67	68	69	65	67	63	70	70
2 June 1997	55	73	69	73	73	66	63	65	59	66	70	59	67
27 November 2000	57.3	72.7	62.6	67.7	64.1	58.1	62.3	62.3	60.1	62.9	52.2 (Nunavut, 54.9)	63.5	60.5

*referendum

The problem of voting inequality, called malapportionment, is caused when the population in electoral districts or constituencies or ridings is significantly unequal. This happens at the federal level even though the boundaries of federal constituencies are redrawn following each ten-year census to deal with population changes. Some degree of malapportionment between urban and rural areas and in the northern territories is usually tolerated because these areas contain far fewer people than metropolitan urban areas. It could be argued that effective representation by an MLA or MP is hampered when constituencies are geographically large. Also, the interests of rural and remote tiny communities would be poorly represented in a legislature or House of Commons if the criterion of population was strictly observed. The MLAs or MPs of large remote ridings have special difficulties as well. The result is, by the criterion of "rep by pop" or "one person one vote," rural and northern populations are over-represented. Voting inequality thus favours political parties with a rural base of support.

To help elected MPs or MLAs in large rural or remote ridings to do their tasks efficiently and effectively, some changes are recommended:

1. Constituents should have the ability to telephone their representative free of long distance charges.
2. Extra allowances for MPs and MLAs to establish more small constituency offices.
3. Generous travel cost allowances for members, including the cost of charter aircraft and rented radio equipped four-wheel drive vehicles.

The legal limit to the amount of difference between

electoral districts both provincial and federal has been twenty-five percent plus or minus of the quotient. The quotient for a province is the population of that province divided by the number of ridings or MLAs. If one riding has twice as many people as another riding then the voters of the less-populated riding would have twice the voting power of the riding with the larger population. The same would be true federally.

The readjustment of federal and most provincial electoral districts is done by independent commissions. The ridings are supposed to correspond, as closely as reasonably possible, to the quotient of each province. But the federal commissions must take into consideration, "the community of interest or community of identity in or the historical pattern of an electoral district... and a manageable geographic size for districts in sparsely populated, rural or northern regions." While generally restricted to the tolerance of 25 percent either way, a commission may exceed this limit, "in circumstances viewed by the commission as being extra-ordinary." This is fraught with danger to democracy and the "one person one vote" concept. Approximating mathematical precision must be the watchword. No other considerations are capable of supplanting the rule of equality of voting power as the fundamental one. Other factors such as history, geography, community interests and the like should be allowed to play a role only on a secondary basis.

Are riding inequalities a violation of the Charter of Rights and Freedoms? Some legal experts believe it is. However, the Supreme Court of Canada has upheld the legislative mandating of non-population factors as distinct from the principles of voting equality under the Charter.

Unequal provincial representation in the House of Commons is a second problem of similar complexity. In Canada, the population in 1998 was 30,300,000. Divide this by 301 constituencies and the quotient is 100,664 people. Ideally, every one of the 301 ridings should have 100,664 individuals and one member of parliament. Obviously, this is impossible because of geographical and urban and rural reasons which have been stated. But again it is a desirable democratic goal under a "one person one vote" or representation by population concept. Let us see how close each province is to that ideal number on the federal scene.

	1998 population	MP Present seats	Rep by pop quotient seats
Newfoundland	544,000	7	5
Prince Edward Island	136,000	4	1
Nova Scotia	935,000	11	9
New Brunswick	753,000	10	7
Quebec	7,333,000	75	73
Ontario	11,412,000	103	113
Manitoba	1,139,000	14	11
Saskatchewan	1,024,000	14	10
Alberta	2,915,000	26	29
British Columbia	4,010,000	34	40
Yukon Territory	32,000	1	1
Northwest Territory	67,000	2	2
		301	301

The figures show that Ontario should have ten more seats, Alberta should have three more and British Columbia should have six more. It can be argued that these inequalities are also a violation of Section 15(1) of the Charter of Rights and Freedoms where all voters should be equal in the eyes of electoral law.

"Every individual is equal before and under the law and

has the right to the equal protection and equal benefit of the law without discrimination and, in particular, without discrimination based on race, national, or ethnic origin, colour, religion, sex, age or mental or physical disability."

Why is the equality of voting power so distorted? How did these aberrations of electoral inequality happen in the House of Commons?

We begin with the 1915 Senatorial or "Grandfather" clause which states that a province cannot have fewer seats in the House of Commons than it does in the Senate. This guarantees that Prince Edward Island will always have at least four seats in the House of Commons.

Next we have the "fifteen percent clause" in which a province could not lose more than fifteen percent of the number of seats to which it had been entitled at the last readjustment regardless of a population decline.

Then we have the Representation Act of 1974 which guaranteed that no province could lose seats but also created a complicated "amalgam" formula.

The Standing Committee on Privileges and Elections in 1974 established that:

"The objective must be adequate and realistic representation of all Canadians bearing in mind the historic undertakings arising out of Confederation and its responsibilities. The allocation of seats (in the House of Commons) is at the very heart of the Confederation compromise."

A "compromise" was thus proposed to deal with representation in the House of Commons. The new formula, the third in Canadian history, was lengthy. As in the pre-1946 rules, Quebec was used as the basis for calculations, but there were three differences. First, Quebec would henceforth be entitled to 75 seats instead of 65. Second, the number of seats assigned to Quebec was to grow by four at each subsequent readjustment in such a manner as to slow down the growth in the average population of an electoral district. Thirdly, three categories of provinces were created: *large* provinces, those having a population of more than 2.5 million, *intermediate* provinces, namely, those with populations between 1.5 million and 2.5 million and *small* provinces, with populations under 1.5 million. Only the large provinces were to be allocated seats in strict proportion to Quebec; separate rules were to apply to the small and intermediate provinces.

Finally, we have the present complicated formula which was instituted in 1985 by another Representation Act. This brought into effect a new "grandfather" clause that guaranteed each province no fewer seats than it had in 1976 or during the 33rd Parliament. The calculation in this case was carried out in the following four steps:

1. Allocation to the territories

Starting with 282 seats that the House of Commons of Canada had in 1985, two seats are allocated to the Northwest Territories and one to the Yukon Territory, leaving 279 seats. This number is used to calculate the electoral quotient.

2. Calculating the electoral district average

The total population of the ten provinces is divided by 279 (the number obtained after allocating seats to the territories) to obtain the electoral quota or quotient, *which is used to determine the number of seats for each province.*

3. Distributing the seats to each province

The theoretical number of seats to be allocated to each province in the House of Commons is calculated by dividing the total population of each province by the quotient obtained in step 2. If the result leaves a remainder higher than 0.50, the number of seats is rounded up to the next whole number.

4. Adjustments

After the theoretical number of seats per province is obtained, adjustments are made in a process referred to as applying the "senatorial clause" and the "grandfather clause."

As we have seen, since 1915, the senatorial clause has guaranteed that no province has fewer members in the House of Commons than it has in the Senate. The Representation Act, 1985, brought into effect a new grandfather clause that guaranteed each province no fewer seats than it had in 1976 or during the 33rd Parliament.

The table (see facing page) shows the formula applied to provincial populations. Notice that Alberta, British Columbia and Ontario are the only provinces not affected by "Special Clauses." No wonder these three provinces are badly underrepresented. It is the adjustments that make inequality in provincial representation.

To correct this electoral imbalance is going to take a lot of work. The bottom line would be a national referendum on the reallocation of seats involving constitutional change. It is highly likely that a referendum of this nature would easily pass because the majority of Canadians would benefit from equality of voting power. One person, one vote or rep. by pop. is the democratic goal.

Another problem that bothers many Canadians is our single member plurality electoral system, sometimes called the "first past the post" arrangement. Under this

Redistribution Formula applied to the 1991 census figures

CALCULATIONS

Province or Territory	No. of seats established in 1976 and constituting 33rd Parliament[1]	Pop 1991	National Quotient[2]	Rounded Result	Special Clauses[3]	Total	Electoral Quotient
Newfoundland	7	568,474	97,532	6	1	7	81,211
Prince Edward Island	4	129,765	97,532	1	3	4	32,441
Nova Scotia	11	899,942	97,532	9	2	11	81,813
New Brunswick	10	723,900	97,532	7	3	10	72,390
Quebec	75	6,895,963	97,532	71	4	75	91,946
Ontario	95	10,084,885	97,532	103	-	103	97,912
Manitoba	14	1,091,942	97,532	11	3	14	77,996
Saskatchewan	14	988,928	97,532	10	4	14	70,638
Alberta	21	2,545,553	97,532	26	-	26	97,906
British Columbia	28	3,282,061	97,532	34	-	34	96,531
Northwest Territories	2	57,649	-	-	-	2	
Yukon Territory	1	27,797	-	-	-	1	
TOTAL	282	27,296,859				301	

1 *Assign two seats to the Northwest Territories and one to the Yukon Territory (three seats).*
2 *Use 279 seats and population of provinces to establish national quotient (27,211,413 ÷ 279 = 97,532).*
3 *Add seats to provinces pursuant to "Senatorial Clause" guarantee in the Constitution and new "Grandfather Clause") based on 33rd Parliament.*
4 *There is no quotient for the Northwest Territories*

method a political party's representation in the House of Commons will depend on how well its candidates fare in the 301 constituency races that make up a general election. The leading party's candidates may account for no more than 40 percent of the popular vote and yet obtain a majority of seats in the Commons. In 1997, 67 percent of Canadians who had the right to vote went to the polls. Of these, 38 percent voted Liberal, 19 percent voted Reform, 19 percent voted Conservative, 11 percent voted for the Bloc, and 11 percent voted for the NDP. So 60 percent voted against the party which became the government. In the November 2000 election the percentages were: Liberals 41 percent, Alliance 26 percent, Conservatives 12 percent, Bloc 11 percent, and NDP 9 percent. Fifty-eight percent thus voted against the governing party.

Some Canadians believe proportional representation is the answer. Usually this is an electoral system by which political parties hold a percentage of seats in the House of Commons or the legislatures which approximates their percentage of the popular vote in the election. For example, a party that wins 40 percent of the popular vote would hold 40 percent of the seats. If this system had been in effect in the 2000 federal election, the Liberals would have 123 seats, not 173 and the Alliance would have 77, not 66. In short, a minority government.

Variants of proportional representation systems are used in many European countries with Great Britain being the exception. In some, electors vote for a list of party candidates in multi-member ridings. This system usually results in no single party winning a majority of seats and governments are formed through coalitions of parties. These coalitions seldom last longer than a year or two.

It is obvious that in our "first past the post" electoral system, the candidate in each riding with the most votes wins and this frequently works out that the majority of the voters did not vote for the winner.

However, proportional representation has many problems. It may be criticized on seven main counts:

First, it promotes a splintering of the party system, encouraging the creation of minority parties that represent very narrow interests and undermining the development of broad-based national parties capable of bridging sectional rivalries and the differences between special interests and advocacy groups.

Second, proportional representation produces unstable government. More minority governments would be elected with subsequent frequent elections. France, Italy and Israel have had this occur. Canada, like many democratic nations, works better with a strong, stable government. Of the thirty-four Canadian governments elected betwen 1867 and 1988, five fell because of a defeat in the House of Commons, leading to an election. In all five cases these were minority governments. Could the Canadian constitution have been patriated if proportional representation had been in effect? Or the Charter of Rights and Freedoms or the flag or any other significant contentious legislative changes? All would have been compromised or dropped in order to obtain support so that the government would not be defeated.

A third criticism of proportional representation is that it encourages ideological polarity and enables extremist parties to gain representation in parliament or legislatures.

A fourth defect of proportional representation is that, in the author's opinion, citizens would feel less motivated to join a political party. If the voter can choose between the candidate of party B or C as well as A, he or she may feel that positive support for one party is inconsequential.

A fifth problem is that proportional representation would tend to send a mixed group of MPs or MLAs to the House of Commons or the Legislative Assemblies. It says that in many ridings citizens were unable to form a consensus on whom to represent them. So, the problem is passed to the House of Commons or provincial assemblies to struggle with on each and every vote.

Another difficulty is that proportional representation would produce permanent coalition governments, which would be preoccupied with obtaining consensus on every issue. Politicians would decide behind closed doors which parties should combine to govern. Multi-party and coalition governments are messy, quarrelsome, inefficient and ineffective in contrast to the clear authority of a majority government.

A final problem is the geographical area that MLAs or MPs would represent. Would remote and rural areas be too large for adequate service by the elected member? Proportional representation thus weakens MP or MLA constituent contact.

At the provincial level, British Columbia (1952 and 1953), Alberta (1926 to 1959) and Manitoba (1920 to 1950) have used preferential ballots. All use the plurality or "first past the post" election system today.

In 1991 the Lortie Commission on Electoral Reform examined our federal electoral system and concluded the following:

"We recommend the continuation of the Canadian system of

single-member constituencies defined in a geographic manner because we consider it the best way to achieve the desired equality and efficacy of the vote within the Canadian system of responsible parliamentary government generally."

A major change in the federal voting system would likely have to be put to the Canadian people in a national referendum. With a number of different proportional representation schemes it would be very difficult to ask a simple question. There is a two-ballot runoff system in which a candidate must obtain 50 percent plus one of the votes; a list system in which there are multi-member ridings and the seats are awarded to the parties based on their respective share of the vote; and a mixed system where the voters elect two groups of MPs. In the last case there is usually a floor of 10 or 20 percent of the vote to obtain seats.

In this chapter a number of recommendations to improve our vote have been made. Several more recommendations are suggested. The first is that political parties not be allowed to receive money from any source except individuals. The prohibition of donations to parties and candidates would apply to organizations of all kinds: to business corporations, trade unions, professional bodies, interest groups and other associations. This would also motivate all political parties to secure more members.

There is a need, too, for individual contributions to be restricted. Most parties have donors of large donations and are given special recognition within the party. These must be limited by law. The legislation would have to be tough. Any offense should be punished by a fine that is levied on both the contributor and on the party or candidate accepting the contribution. An independent commission would investigate and impose fines. If there is political will, legislation can be enacted and enforced.

A second suggestion is that advocacy or interest third-party advertising should be prohibited during an election campaign. The election campaign is a contest between parties conducted under rules to ensure that the contest is as fair as possible. Before or after, interest or advocacy groups can try to shape people's views. During a campaign, democracy must come first. The battle for votes should be between the parties and candidates seeking to take on the responsibilities of government. The Elections Act was revised in May of 2000. Happily, third-party advertising is now restricted. A third party is a person or group other than the candidate, a registered political party, or its electoral district association.

To publicize the changes, Elections Canada ran full-page ads across Canada in September, 2000.

> *"Third party advertising:*
> *New rules apply to third parties who advertise during an election to promote or oppose a candidate, a political party or the leader of a political party, or to state their positions on an issue with which a registered party or candidate is associated.*
> *A third party must report all contributions received for the purpose of election advertising up to six months before the election was called, the name and address of every such contributor who gave more than $200, and all advertising expenses during the election period.*
> *A third party cannot use foreign or anonymous contributions for election advertising.*
> *A third party must identify itself in all election ads.*

A third party that spends $500 or more in election advertising must register with the Chief Electoral Officer and appoint a financial agent.
A third party that spends $500 or more must appoint an auditor.
A third party can spend no more than $3000 on any single electoral district, and no more than $150,000 in total."

The Supreme Court, on November 10, 2000, in an eight-to-one decision, overturned an injunction that would have suspended the above regulations. The court said the rules regulating spending would, "permit all voices during an election to be heard fairly."

This author agrees with the court. After the election or before it is called, third parties can advertise without limit. What they wish to do is influence elections without taking any responsibility. For example, in the 1997 election, a group called APEC ran full-page ads across Canada, except in Quebec, saying "The Liberals, Conservatives and New Democrats all favour Distinct Society status for Quebec. Do not vote for them."

To summarize, our votes become more democratically responsible when:

1. More citizens join a political party.
2. More citizens vote in elections.
3. There is a stricter adherence to the "one person one vote" principle.
4. There is representation by population in the House of Commons and in provincial legislatures.
5. There is representation by population in the Senate (see Chapter Four).
6. Restricted donations are made to political parties only by individuals.

CHAPTER THREE
Our Referendums

"The greatest happiness of the greatest number is the foundation of all morals and legislation."
Jeremy Bentham 1748–1832 (English philosopher)

All modern democracies are representative democracies. Government at all levels is carried out by elected individuals who represent the people who elected them. Citizens delegate authority to their representatives, holding them responsible for their actions through periodic elections. Representative democracies sometimes include decision-making processes that provide opportunities for greater and more frequent citizen participation than voting every few years. Referendums, also called plebiscites, are direct votes of citizens on public questions and allow for widespread citizen participation in public affairs.

Referendums have been used for many years by cities to have citizens vote on such matters as the funding of major public works. Parliament's consultation of Canadian citizens has only been done three times since Confederation: on prohibition in 1898, on conscription in 1942 (when four out of five voters in Ontario supported conscription and four out of five Quebecers opposed it) and on the 1992 Charlottetown Accord (which cost almost the same amount as an election—$165 million).

In all Canadian provinces except Quebec, referendums have never been a regular procedure. In the 1991 British Columbia provincial election the electors answered two referendum questions: "Should voters be given the right to propose questions that the government of British Columbia must submit to voters by referendum?" This was a proposal of "initiative" used by many American states to provide a system by which a predetermined number of voters can put an issue on the ballot and subject it to a binding vote. In British Columbia, 83 percent voted in favour.

The second question was, "Should voters be given the right to vote between elections for the removal of their member of the Legislative Assembly?" This is a system of "recall" which enables a specific number of voters to require that their MLA resign and run in a by-election. On this question 81 percent voted in favour.

The actual procedures that the British Columbia government instituted to legalize "initiative" and "recall" were so complicated that neither has been carried out.

Obviously there must be stringent rules to prevent abuses by interest groups and also to stop supporters of a defeated candidate from the recall of the election winner.

At the national level, consider the difficulty of having referendums on the legalization of marijuana, the death penalty, abortion, childcare, fishing quotas, free trade, tax reform, gun control, etcetera.

In spite of this, many Canadians feel left out of the political process or think that governments do not reflect their values and priorities and so believe referendums are a good idea. It will empower them, they believe, by turning politicians into quasi servants—forcing them to keep in touch with and be accountable to their voters.

But frequent referendums could hinder the ability of governments to pursue a planned set of policies. Voters may find it difficult to decide on complex issues like the ones listed above. They also may be influenced by lobbyists, pollsters, fundraisers, interest groups and advertising agencies who, in some instances, would be willing to spend millions of dollars. Voters may find it difficult to decide on complex issues like free trade and there is a possibility that contradictory proposals would be approved. The repeated use of referendums could lead to voter fatigue and result in low turnout at the polls. Nationally, referendums could produce skewed results regionally leading to minorities imposing their values on the majority in some areas. For the latter reason it has been proposed that in any referendum a double-majority stipulation be included. That is, for a referendum to pass it must have 50 percent plus one support generally plus majority support in each region. This would add a further complication to a complex procedure. For example, if a referendum on a triple E senate was voted on and passed by a majority, Quebec could defeat it by voting "no."

Former *Financial Post* editor Diane Francis advocates, "routine referendums on major social and economic issues." This statement indicates a lack of understanding of the difficulties of such a process. Imagine a referendum question on social spending versus a reduction of the national debt. This is politics of inclusion carried to absurdity. Referendums should be used as a measure of last resort, except for constitutional change, and real leaders do not need to rely on them to take political action.

Of all the countries of the world only Switzerland uses a binding referendum as a device in the regular operation of its central government.

Certainly, in Canada, legislation by referendum is not seen by many as an alternative to representative democracy. In short, you don't democratize the House of Commons or provincial legislatures by referendums.

It is true, however, that Canadians are no longer going to accept elite decisions on constitutional changes coming from the cabinet or federal-provincial agreements. The procedure must be on representation and legitimization through popular consultation and referendums, as difficult as this is to do.

Constitutional changes by referendum must be crystal clear and simple. The Charlottetown Accord was endorsed by Brian Mulroney, Jean Chretien, Audrey McLaughlin and their parties, all provincial parties, two territorial leaders, four aboriginal leaders, and the Canadian Labour Congress. Yet a majority of 54 percent of Canadians voted "No."

It was rejected because it was too complex a constitutional revision. If it had concerned itself only with Senate reform it would have likely passed. Outside Quebec, Canadians voted "No" because it offered Quebec too much and inside Quebec, citizens were negative because it did not offer Quebec enough.

So what we need in Canada is not more leadership but more partnership, more participation in constitutional decisions that will bring about a more democratic Canada. Constitutional change through referendum will provide for such participation (see Chapter Five).

As Senate reform is probably advocated by more Canadians than any other constitutional issue it will be dealt with in the next chapter.

CHAPTER FOUR
Our Senate

"It would be idle to deny that the Senate has not fulfilled the hopes of its founders; and it is well also to remember that the hopes of its founders were not excessively high."
—McGregor Dawson (Canadian historian)

Section 25 of the Constitution Act of 1867 established an upper chamber in Canada. Because, at that time, our country did not have a leisure class and aristocratic traditions like England, the Fathers of Confederation opted for a non-hereditary appointed Senate. Thus a senator is not born into the Senate but has usually influenced his way in at the pleasure of the Prime Minister.

Our Canadian Senate of 104 persons is mostly filled by those who enjoy rewards for past services to a party—not to Canada or the Canadian people. Canadian democracy is cheated by this "stagnant wading pool for the plumpest of the Canadian fat-cats to splash in." (Larry Zolt, page 17 in *Survival of the Fattest*).

Another writer, Claire Hoy, in his book *Nice Work*, says Canadians see the Senate "as a useless, expensive, undemocratic appendage of government and as a refuge and dumping ground for bagmen, party apologists and failed politicians." His book goes on to give a history of Senate appointments and Senate work over the years in all its absenteeism, legalized bribery and shabbiness.

Canadians pay more than fifty million dollars a year for our Senate. In 2000, senators got $64,000 annually plus a $10,000 tax-free allowance and many perks. The Senate sits only three days a week and in 1997 held just fifty-six sittings.

As it is a non-elective body, it really has no place in our democratic society because it is a party institution not a people institution. We are stuck with it and major reform such as a Triple E Senate (elected, equal and effective) or total abolition seems remote.

Naturally, Quebec would oppose a referendum on abolition of the Senate or one which would reduce its number of senators. Quebec power is weakened in the federal government every time a province like British Columbia or Ontario is granted more MPs. Because of this, Quebec would not allow a decrease by a constitutional referendum of the number of senators from Quebec, just as it would fight a national referendum on Quebec secession.

Fortunately, the Senate is a minor partner in the process of parliamentary government. Some of the activities of the Senate are useful even though it has none of the real powers of the elected American Senate. Our Senate is a sober second thought on legislation coming from the House of Commons. It also scrutinizes the work of executive agencies and considers private bills. Since 1868, suggestions have been made for Senate reform. Rarely has this come from the Prime Minister and rarer still from the Senators themselves.

Practically all appointments by Prime Ministers have gone to political supporters of the government who remain loyal after their appointments. Naturally, the tendency of the Senate to amend government bills increases when the majority of senators do not belong to the government's party in the House of Commons. Prime Ministers would thus not like to have changes which could result in legislative delays of this nature.

Trudeau once offered to allow the provinces one-half of all senatorial appointments but did not follow this up. A senate committee suggested that senators not be allowed to attend party caucuses so that they would then be less partisan. This idea died. In the matter of an elected Senate, the Supreme Court of Canada was not helpful. It stated that election would impair the function of the senate as "a thoroughly independent body which could canvass dispassionately the measures of the House of Commons." Could it be argued that the Senate, filled by political patronage on an appointive basis does that? The answer is a resounding "No."

In 1979 Bill C-60 proposed that the Senate should be made up of one-half of members chosen by the House of Commons and one-half of members chosen by the provincial legislatures (a House of Federation). The Supreme Court ruled that Parliament could not abolish the senate and replace it with another body.

Later a Senate committee suggested that every second appointment to the Senate be made from a list submitted by appropriate provincial or territorial governments. This proposal, like so many others, died from inertia.

Another Senate problem is the gross representation inequalities in the provincial apportionment of senators. In 1867 the Fathers of Confederation opted for representation by region rather then by province. Ontario, Quebec and the Maritimes were all given 24 seats. In 1915 Western Canada was designated a region and assigned 24 seats—six to each of the four provinces: British Columbia, Alberta, Saskatchewan and Manitoba. As a condition of entering Confederation, Newfoundland–Labrador was given six seats in 1949.

Based on 1991 census population figures, the distribution of Senate seats looks like this:

Province	Number of Senate seats	Population per Senator
Newfoundland	6	94,745
Prince Edward Island	4	32,411
Nova Scotia	10	88,994
New Brunswick	10	72,390
Quebec	24	287,331
Ontario	24	420,204
Manitoba	6	181,990
Saskatchewan	6	164,821
Alberta	6	424,259
British Columbia	6	547,010
Yukon	1	27,797
Northwest Territories	1	57,649

The unfairness of this representation is obvious. Representation by population it is not!

Claire Hoy suggests a reduced elected Senate of 67 members: twelve each from Ontario and Quebec, seven each from British Columbia and Alberta, five each from Manitoba, Saskatchewan, New Brunswick and Nova Scotia, four from Newfoundland–Labrador, two from Prince Edward Island and three from the Territories. This idea would require a major constitutional change to which Quebec would never agree.

Is it possible to make our Canadian Senate more democratic without a major constitutional change? The answer lies in making incremental improvements which would not run the risk of a veto by a large province.

First, with regard to representation inequalities: The four Western Provinces had a 1998 population of 9,088,000 (British Columbia: 4,010,000, Alberta: 2,915,000, Saskatchewan: 1,024,000, Manitoba: 1,139,000) and the four Atlantic Provinces a 1998 population of 2,368,000 (Nova Scotia: 10 seats, 753,000, Prince Edward Island: 4 seats, 136,000, Newfoundland-Labrador: 6 seats, 544,000) with Ontario at 11,412,000. In a constitutional amendment under the general formula requiring consent of the Senate, the House of Commons and seven provincial legislatures representing 50 percent of Canada's population, the thirty Atlantic Provinces Senate seats would be reduced to 14 (New Brunswick: 5, Nova Scotia: 5, P.E.I.: 1, Newfoundland–Labrador: 3) with the four Western provinces increased to 36 (B.C.: 14, Alberta: 12, Saskatchewan: 5, Manitoba: 5) and Ontario augmented to 28. This new arrangement could be done over a period of, say, ten years and would yield the same number of Senators as we now have. Thus Quebec would not lose power in the Senate.

An elected Senate, it is suggested by this author, could be done without a constitutional amendment. Parliament could move unilaterally to permit provinces to elect Senators. This author further recommends that elections of Senators coincide with provincial elections and that those who have been elected by the registered voters of each province serve for a period of ten years or until they reach the age of 75. This would allow the Senate to regularly rejuvenate itself.

It is important to realize that Canada is the only nation

in the world in which senators are all appointed by a central government so a fairer system should be a national priority.

Major constitutional Senate reform on its more effective role brings with it many problems. For example, finding agreement on the role and functions of the Senate might require the House of Commons to relinquish some of its existing powers.

This chapter on our Senate concludes that major change such as an abolition of the Senate or a Triple E Senate is not feasible at this time but that reforms on representation equality and election of senators is realizable. As amending our constitution is part of major Senate changes, the next chapter will deal with that subject.

CHAPTER FIVE
Amending Our Constitution

"The existence of a constitution does not by itself ensure that politics is democratic."
—Stephen Brooks, University of Windsor

Differences of opinion on the constitution between the federal government and the provinces started soon after Confederation and has continued for over 135 years.

In 1867 the Act of Confederation which was officially called the British North America Act was ratified by the British Parliament and became effective July 1 of that year. It was an agreement between New Brunswick, Nova Scotia, Quebec and Ontario to create a new level of government that would have certain powers and divided legislative power between the provinces and the federal government. The Act did not specifically define all divisions of power and there were parts of it that allowed for interpretations in favour of federal power or in favour of provincial power.

John A. Macdonald, our first Prime Minister, wanted a strong federal government. Under his leadership, the government intervened regularly in provincial affairs by means of a disallowance clause which permitted him to quash any provincial law that he deemed to be contrary to the national interest. Between 1867 and 1896 the federal government used this power on more than sixty occasions, much to the irritation of the provinces.

In Quebec, two concepts gradually emerged. The first was that the federal government had been brought into being by the provinces and, for that reason, should not be subject to it. The second was that French Canadians had only one government that really spoke for them, and that was the provincial one.

In 1896 Wilfred Laurier became Prime Minister and he was more open to the idea of provincial autonomy. However, in 1912, the federal government introduced "conditional grants" in which large sums of money were given to the provinces to be used for specific needs, previously determined by the federal government.

World War One benefited the federal government's power as it introduced corporate taxes and personal income taxes as "temporary" taxes which were not subsequently abolished. This angered the provinces and taxes became a battleground between the federal and provincial governments which continues down to this day.

In the 1930s the depression forced provincial governments to ask the federal government for help in setting up social security and public works programs.

In 1935 the provinces agreed to let the Constitution be modified so that Mackenzie King could legally establish an unemployment insurance program which was introduced in 1941. It was a cornerstone of the federal welfare state and was a significant step towards a strong federal government.

After World War Two the federal government convened federal-provincial conferences to attempt to convince provinces to cede power in areas of taxes, education and social programs.

In 1951, after obtaining the consent of all provinces, the federal government modified the Constitution to ensure that it had a monopoly on old-age pensions.

"Opting out" was granted in 1960 to all provinces by which any province could refuse to take part in a federal-provincial shared-cost program. Instead, it could set up its own program and still receive funding from the federal government.

When the first Trudeau government (1968–1971) took office, the issue of a constitutional amending formula became basically a battle of a decentralized government versus a strong centralized one. A series of seven federal-provincial constitutional conferences were held from 1968 to 1971. At the 1971 Victoria conference an amending formula was finally agreed upon. Constitutional amendments would require the approval of two Atlantic provinces, Ontario, Quebec and two western provinces with the majority of the population of western Canada.

Despite the unanimity that was achieved, the agreement was never implemented because again Quebec withdrew its consent. Premier Bourassa and Premier Lasage before him showed Canadians that agreement among first ministers is not a guarantee that change will proceed. Public debate and public opinion have a role to play after a first ministers' conference and before confirmation by legislatures.

In 1975–1976 Trudeau tried once more but the provinces insisted that some federal government powers be changed in their favour.

The spring of 1980 saw the first Quebec referendum campaign and a victory for the federalists. After this Trudeau again tried to find an acceptable amending formula but he insisted that the national interest must prevail over regional interests. His government introduced a constitutional resolution in the House of Commons in October of 1980 giving two years to reach an agreement on an amending formula. If that failed the Victoria amending formula would prevail with a provision for a national referendum to break deadlocks. Eight provinces objected and proposed an amending formula where there would not be a veto from any province and all provinces would be considered equal.

Surprisingly, René Levesque signed the document. It provided for amendments with the consent of seven provinces representing more than fifty percent of the population of Canada. Where the rights of any particular province were affected and, if a province disagreed with the amendment, such a province would be allowed to opt out with full fiscal compensation.

Finally, after much negotiation and concessions, except for Quebec, the federal government agreed that seven provinces (two-thirds) with fifty percent of the population could approve constitutional amendments—the so-called 7/50 formula. Provinces could opt out of constitutional change affecting their powers but there would be no fiscal compensation. For a limited number of matters including a change to the amending formula itself, unanimity was required.

On that amending formula the Constitution Act of 1982

came into effect without Quebec. The first effort at amending the constitution, using the 1982 rules, ended in acrimonious failure. The proposed amendment was in fact a group of changes collectively known as the Meech Lake Accord. The Accord was a 1987 agreement between Prime Minister Brian Mulroney and the ten provincial premiers in response to a series of five demands that the Quebec government of Robert Bourassa wanted met before it was willing to sign the 1981 agreement that produced the Constitution Act, 1982. The main changes proposed by the Meech Lake Accord included the following:

1. *Immigration policy.* Some federal powers over immigration would be transferred to Quebec. This would have entrenched in the constitution an agreement that had been reached between Ottawa and Quebec in 1978. Any other province would also be able to assume these expanded powers.
2. *Distinct society.* Quebec would be recognized as a "distinct society," and the government and legislature of that province would have a responsibility to "preserve and promote the distinct identity of Quebec." The distinct identity referred to in this section was explicitly linked to the French language. As well, this section of the Accord declared that the constitution of Canada shall be interpreted in a manner consistent with the recognition of Quebec as a distinct society.
3. *Supreme Court.* Provincial governments would have the right to nominate candidates for the Supreme Court of Canada. When filling a vacancy on the Court, Ottawa would be obliged to select from the provinces' lists of nominees and to select from the Quebec government's list of nominees in the case of the three Supreme Court

positions that must be filled by members of the Quebec bar.
4. *Shared-cost programs.* Any provincial government would have the right to receive reasonable compensation from Ottawa in the event that it decided not to participate in a new national shared-cost program. The only stipulation was that the provincial program would have to be "compatible with the national objectives."
5. *Amending procedures.* Two important changes were proposed to the amending procedures. The first would have changed the opting-out provision, so that a dissenting province would be entitled to reasonable compensation to finance its own programs in the case of any transfer of legislative powers from the provinces to Ottawa. The second change involved the list of subjects requiring unanimous consent of the provinces. The Accord would have doubled the length of this list, adding to it Senate reform, the principle of proportionate representation of the provinces in the House of Commons, any change to the Supreme Court of Canada, and both the extension of existing provinces into the territories and the establishment of new provinces.

After three years of wrangling marked by both an anti-French backlash in parts of English Canada and a revival of separatist nationalism in Quebec, the Accord expired. It was not ratified by all of the provincial legislatures before the three-year deadline imposed on the process by the constitution.

Prime Minister Mulroney and some of the provincial premiers had insisted that the Meech Lake Accord could not be altered in any respect. It was submitted to the legislatures for ratification, not modification.

The next attempt to change the constitution was the Charlottetown Accord. On August 28, 1992, Brian Mulroney, ten premiers, two territorial leaders and leaders of First Nations agreed to another Constitutional Accord. This "Son of Meech" was voted on by Canadians in a referendum on October 26, 1992. Terms of the Accord were:

1. A Canada clause listing the fundamental characteristics of Canadian society;
2. Recognition of Quebec as a distinct society;
3. Entrenchment of the right to aboriginal self-government;
4. An elected Senate with equal representation from the provinces and, eventually, special seats for aboriginal representatives;
5. Francophone veto in the Senate regarding bills affecting the French language or culture;
6. Guarantee of three Quebec judges on the Supreme Court and provincial input in the selection of judges;
7. Quebec guaranteed at least 25 percent of the seats in the House of Commons;
8. Entrenchment of Ottawa's right to spend money on matters within provincial jurisdiction, but with the provision that any province could opt out of any new shared-cost program and be entitled to reasonable compensation to run its own program;
9. Confirmation of the provinces' exclusive jurisdiction in several policy areas, and some decentralization of powers to the provinces in the areas of immigration and labour policy.

The referendum question asked was: "Do you agree that the Constitution of Canada should be renewed on the basis of the agreement reached on August 28, 1992?"

The majority of Canadians (54.5 percent) rejected the reforms. Many English Canadians voted "no" to the Charlottetown Accord because they thought it gave Quebec too much and many Francophone Quebecers rejected it because they believed it gave them too little. Prime Minister Mulroney did not help by calling opponents of the Accord, "enemies of Canada." He had given the provinces most of what the premiers asked for and demanded nothing in return. As the late Pierre Trudeau said to the Senate in 1988: "How do you make a country stronger by weakening the only government that can talk for all Canadians?"

On October 30, 1995, the people of Quebec narrowly rejected sovereignty-association, with 50.6 percent of the votes going to the "No" side and 49.4 percent going to the "Yes" side.

So, for the last 135 years there has been interest by Canadians in our constitution. The biggest problem, as we have seen, is in making rules for changes to that document. Those attempts have been a frustrating endeavour. The United States has had similar problems. Since 1789 over 9000 amendments have been proposed. Only 33 have made it through Congress to be put to the states. Only 26 have been ratified (prohibition and its repeal cancelled each other out).

Thus, Canadian citizens may look forward to few constitutional changes in this new century in spite of the fact that the relationship of the federal government and the provinces bears little relationship to what it was at Confederation.

AMENDING OUR CONSTITUTION

One thing is sure. Changes in our constitution must be accomplished not by the manipulation of constitutional issues by the national government and provinces but by a broad Canadian public consensus in support of amendments which result in fairness and better democracy. The argument that many Canadians are tired of constitutional concerns should not be allowed to deter reforms. Neither does the debate represent "old Canada" (the East) versus "new Canada" (the West).

However, the complexity of amending the constitution is illustrated by a table from page 175 of Stephen Brook's book, *Canadian Democracy* (see next page).

The above procedures for constitutional amendment show that Canadians who are the source of sovereignty lack the power to bring about change because it lies with a combination of federal and provincial governments. However, the Charlottetown referendum established a convention requiring a national referendum before any significant constitutional change is made. This opens a new path for constitutional change.

In view of all this, how then are we to improve our constitutional amending formula? There seems to be few acceptable answers—only perplexing problems. And these problems pose excruciating dilemmas where standing still is undemocratic and movement in any direction is blocked by inertia, prejudice, power struggles and popular resistance. The challenge is to modernize our Constitution to prepare Canada to meet the needs of the twenty-first century.

In this writer's view the American amendment formula could be adapted in part for Canada. No veto, no unanimity. Seventy-five percent approval vote in the House of

AMENDING OUR CONSTITUTION

Procedure	Requirement	Application
1. General (ss. 38, 42)	Resolution passed by the House of Commons and the Senate Two-thirds of the legislatures of the provinces that together comprise at least half the population of all the provinces (the so-called 7/50 formula)	Reduction or elimination of powers, rights, or privileges of provincial governments or legislatures Proportionate representation of the provinces in the House of Commons Senate Supreme Court of Canada (except its composition) Extension of existing provinces into the territories Creation of new provinces
2. Unanimous consent (s. 41)	Resolution passed by the House of Commons and the Senate* Resolution passed by every provincial legislature (veto)	Queen Governor General Lieutenant-governors Right of each province to at least as many seats in the House of Commons as it has in the Senate Use of the English or French language (except changes that apply only to a single province) Composition of the Supreme Court Changing the amending procedures of the Constitution
3. Ottawa and one or more of the provinces (s. 43)	Resolution passed by the House of Commons and the Senate* Resolution passed by the legislature of each province where the amendment applies	Alteration of boundaries between provinces Use of French or English in a particular province or territory
4. Ottawa or a province acting alone (ss. 44, 45)	If Ottawa, a resolution passed by the House of Commons and the Senate* If a province, a resolution passed by its legislature	Executive government of Canada, the Senate, and the House of Commons, subject to the limits established by ss. 41 and 42 of the Constitution Act, 1982

*If after 180 days the Senate has not passed a resolution already passed by the House of Commons, Senate approval is not necessary.

Commons and Senate, plus seven provincial legislature approvals involving fifty percent of the population of Canada. Or, if necessary, a national referendum approving the change.

This author further proposes the following resolution for the House of Commons to adopt.

Whereas the 1992 Referendum Act permits referendums on constitutional matters in which amendments may be voted on by registered Canadian voters, and

Whereas the most efficient way of having a referendum vote is in conjunction with a federal election vote.

Therefore, be it resolved that a standing all party committee of the House of Commons draw up a number of clear simple amendments and submit them to parliament for approval in a free vote.

Be it further resolved that at appropriate federal elections, a parliamentary approved referendum question on a constitutional amendment be included.

Here are some possible amendments that the House of Commons could approve:

1. Abolition of the "notwithstanding clause." (Section 33 of the Charter of Rights and Freedoms)

This allows provincial and federal legislatures to enact legislation that violates, limits or overrides specific sections of the Charter: fundamental freedoms (s. 2), legal rights (ss. 7-14), and equality rights (s. 15). The notwithstanding clause, or legislative override, does not apply to democratic rights (ss. 3-5), mobility rights (s. 6) or linguistic rights, including minority-language educational rights (ss. 16-23).

The inclusion of section 33 in the Charter in 1982 was a compromise between some provincial premiers, who wanted the principle of parliamentary sovereignty to prevail over otherwise constitutionally entrenched Charter rights, and the Charter's main advocate, Liberal Prime Minister Pierre Trudeau. The notwithstanding clause was expected to be used only as an emergency. When expressly invoked, a law operates notwithstanding the circumvented sections of the Charter for only five years, or for a shorter period if specified, subject to legislative debate and reenactment which is also limited to five years.

The section was invoked by a Conservative government in Saskatchewan in 1986 to compel striking public employees to return to work, and in Quebec, first by the Parti Quebecois government routinely, as that province's National Assembly had not approved the Charter's adoption. The successor Liberal government abandoned the routine invocation of section 33, but used it effectively and significantly to protect revised sections of Quebec's official-language policy on commercial signage. The Supreme Court ruled the earlier law was a violation of the Charter's section 2, freedom of expression, and might have ruled against the revised law as well. The Court had earlier ruled against the province's language law respecting education, as a violation of section 23 which is beyond the reach of section 33.

2. Elimination of the "grandfather clause" relating to MPs in which no province can have fewer seats than it had in 1976.
3. Repeal of the "senatorial clause" in which a province can have no fewer MPs than senators.
4. Withdrawal of the 1974 Representation Act by which no province can lose seats.

5. A constitutional amendment which would make any provincial referendum involving sovereignty association or independence *ultra vires*.
6. No provincial dissent on constitutional amendments.
7. All amendments to apply without financial compensation.

After all, constitutions belong to the people—not politicians. The latter have shown a consistent reluctance to submit constitutional amendments to the people. Therefore, in our Canadian democratic society, referendums should be used to make "amending the constitution" changes.

CHAPTER SIX
Our Patronage

"We are going to be governed whether we like it or not; it is up to us to see to it that we are governed no worse than is absolutely avoidable. We must therefore concern ourselves with politics, as Pascal said, to mitigate as far as possible the damage done by the madness of our rulers."

—Pierre Trudeau

This will be the shortest chapter in the book because patronage in both provincial and federal appointments is the most undemocratic of Canada's policies. It must be eliminated in this present century.

Let us begin with the Governor-General and the Lieutenant-Governors—the most expensive appointments. In both figurehead positions cabinet executive decisions are "rubber-stamped." These well-paying jobs should be advertised, applied for, and approved by the House of Commons for Governor-General and the provincial legislatures for the Lieutenant-Governor. Recall that the important task of Speaker of the House of Commons was formerly appointed by the Prime Minister but reforms in the 1980s gave MPs the right to elect the Speaker in a secret ballot.

Next we have the judiciary. Under the Canadian constitution the Prime Minister has the power to appoint all nine justices of the Supreme Court. No one can challenge these appointments or insist on a review of them. He also appoints all chief justices of all courts. This tends to result in the politicization and deterioration of our justice system. Supreme Court judges earn $175,000 a year and do not need to retire until age 75.

It is strange that, when selecting juries, lawyers are given a number of vetoes so that unacceptable individuals can be eliminated. This is done to protect the accused from jurors who have prejudices or who have a conflict of interest in terms of those on trial or the subject matter involved. But the judge has never had his or her opinions, prejudices or personal life examined. What is required of juries should be required of judges. Surely it would be in the best interest of democracy to have some type of public hearing process for these judicial appointments.

Appointed judges are supposedly "independent" but they incline the courts towards protection of the status quo and represent values that they have accumulated over a long time. As Maurice Duplessis once said, "The Supreme Court is like the Tower of Pisa—it always leans the same way." If applications for judgeships were submitted to an all party committee of the House of Commons or to the provincial legislatures, it would, in the long run, result in a better, more democratic judicial system necessary to meet changing circumstances in a modern Canadian society.

To make matters worse at the federal level, the Charter of Rights and Freedoms has tended to shift power from the House of Commons to the Supreme Court. The latter spends one quarter of its time just dealing with Charter cases. It is thus more important to know the beliefs and values of the nine judges.

In the federal political sphere, the Prime Minister appoints all privy councillors (cabinet ministers), deputy heads of departments and senators. The last was dealt with in Chapter 4.

In addition, he appoints persons to the National Parole Board (45 full-time members and an unlimited number of part-timers), the Citizenship Court (judges), the National Transportation Agency (nine full-time and six part-time members), the International Joint Commission (three commissioners), the Immigration and Refugee Board (95 full-time members), the Atomic Energy of Canada Limited (11 directors), and the National Energy Board (nine permanent members and six temporary members).

Other important appointments include:

The Canadian Radio-television and Telecommunications Commission, the Security Intelligence Review Committee, the Canadian Ports Corporation, the Canadian National Railway, VIA Rail, the Export Development Corporation, the Bank of Canada, Canada Post, the National Capital Commission, the Advisory Council on the Status of Women, the National Arts Centre, the Employment Insurance Referee Chairpersons (part-time), the Auditor-General, and the Access-to-Information Commissioner.

All these positions should be handled by the Civil Service Commission. The jobs should be advertised, applied for and awarded to applicants on the basis of qualifications and merit.

Appointments to important positions such as the Governor of the Bank of Canada, Chairperson of CBC, the Ethics Commissioner and the head of the National Transportation Agency should be based on public hearings and confirmed by an all party committee of the House of Commons. In addition, all these heads should be responsible to the House of Commons.

It is worth noting that the Ethics Commissioners in all of the ten provinces operate independently of the premiers. They also deliver their reports to the legislatures. Stephen Owen, elected as a B.C. Liberal MP in the last federal election, says the federal government needs an independent ombudsman who would oversee the ethics of cabinet ministers as well as handle citizens' complaints about government. "I don't think there is anything more disarming than openness, and the corollery of that is that nothing raises more suspicion than secrecy," Owen said. His model would create a federal ombudsman who would report to Parliament and would preside over a series of deputies, encompassing the current offices of the commissioners for privacy, access to information, and official languages. There would be created a "director of public accountability" in each federal department and Crown corporation. These directors would investigate complaints and forward conclusions to the federal ombudsman.

It should be remembered that Pierre Trudeau made 225 appointments in his final six weeks in office and Brian Mulroney made a total of 665 appointments in a time frame of less than a year.

The patronage that is evident in so many appointments contributes to a loss of confidence by Canadians in our political system.

Disenchantment with our patronage system tends to make Canadians skeptical of politics generally. To reduce patronage a well-designed parliamentary or legislature all party committee structure should be created. This would give MPs and MLAs more power, reduce partisanship and promote serious examination of appointments. This Standing Committee would play a public role in advertising, interviewing and choosing individuals. Openness and transparency should be the cornerstone of all selections. The cobwebs and mould of the past must be swept away and open, democratic recruitment put in its place.

CHAPTER SEVEN
Our News Media and Our Political Polls

"Private capitalists inevitably control, directly or indirectly, the main sources of information."
—Albert Einstein

Telecommunications technologies—computers, satellites, televisions, telephones and radios—are breaking down the age old barriers of time and distance. These devices make governments more responsive to the people and make for a more informed electorate.

But there is also a danger that the news media may use these methods in ways that do not truly inform and do not promote the public good.

Journalists have a difficult task in writing political news. To truly understand the political system, they should be card-carrying members of a party. But if they did this, their reporting would obviously not be impartial or objective.

Most reporters simply go to "experts" or politicians to get stories but their articles are frequently derisive, critical and lack an appreciation of the political sincerity of individuals. On the whole the media people believe the public is cynical of politics and interpret news that reflects that point of view. Reporting has often become more designed to affect people's feelings about issues rather than their understanding. The media have become less a collection of similarly employed persons competing independently and more a fellowship representing a narrow range of viewpoints.

As an example, Michael Campbell, columnist for the *Vancouver Sun* recently wrote:

"What is it about forming a government that makes individuals ignore even basic principles of integrity?

When faced with situations that are potentially dangerous to their careers, they regularly respond with a barrage of rationalizations, talk of media conspiracies and glib denials.

Only in politics is such profound lack of courage and integrity celebrated. Many colleagues in the media will excuse the behaviour as being "just politics."

That simply doesn't wash with me. We have elected an avalanche of bystanders who have shown no indication that they have any bottom line other than their political well-being.

I say that's not good enough. What do you say? Have you had enough yet, or are you holding out for your government grant (read: payoff)?"

This columnist represents some of the media who feel that the more they cater to public political cynicism the greater the effect they will have.

Fair, accurate, independent journalism is vital to any democracy and in Canada most is responsible. In reporting political news, however, individual and corporate biases, cultural preconceptions, the imperative of deadlines, and the demands of advertisers often affect the choice of news and how it is covered. An executive of Hollinger Incorporated, David Radler, stated on Peter Gzowski's *Morningside* program on October 17, 1992, "Editors who work for us have the right to voice their opinions after they have stopped working for us."

Owners of news media and editors frequently hire people who have political views similar to their own. Pro-business tendencies of the corporate media are a force that shapes news and limits the diversity of opinions.

On the other side of this issue are the political parties who increasingly try to manage the news to make a politician's actions sound more impressive. With political parties in an election, media handling is done by "spin doctors" who try to give favourable viewpoints to the media.

Obviously, the success of every politician owes a great deal to his or her image—an image created largely by the news media. The danger is that image and style will replace substance and policy.

The importance of a politician's image possibly explains why the media makes much of any stumble or mistake a politician makes. It is modern "gotcha" journalism that often takes minor errors (physical or mental) and blows them up to enormous significance.

It is a truism that there is no such thing as value-free reporting. However, there must be an honest attempt at responsible and competent communication. Politicians have a right to question the escalating power of journalism because in a democracy like Canada power ultimately lies with public opinion. The media tell the public whether the political story is good or bad or worthy or unworthy.

Frequently the headline writers overstate the significance of a political event. Another truism is that fair coverage never gets an award.

The public, too, has a right to free expression and exchange of information uninfluenced by private or public power. In the words of the Statement of Principles of the Canadian Daily Newspapers Association, "It is to report comprehensively, accurately and fairly." The reality is that often the media have little business incentive to incur the cost involved in fulfilling the above objective.

Also the media argues that they are but mirrors of the surrounding reality and just observe and chronicle. The people who are reported upon make the news.

But the media is not just picking up messages here and delivering them there. They select, from the thousands available every day, those messages they decide the public should have. Next they determine how much or how little information on the subject will be used—how many seconds worth of television and radio time, how many inches of type. Then they resolve how the information should be interpreted. Briefly, the message the media delivers is the media's message.

In his book *Birds of a Feather*, Alan Fotheringham says, "Implicit in the love-hate relationship between press and politicians is a marriage—a marriage between two partners who need each other. The politicians need the press for coverage, to manipulate them, to use them as a twisted mirror. The press need the politicians for they are the meal ticket, the reason for existence."

This cynical statement seems to place more blame on the politicians which is what you might expect from a journalist.

But there is still much goodness and fairness in democratic politics. It is sometimes hushed up by the press as if it were shameful to admit it. Integrity is square and honesty is relative. These human conditions are not "cool" in many reporters' minds.

For a number of journalists to be anti-authority is the correct attitude. Politicians who are wealthy are suspect and those who are in positions of power got there by selfish ambition. And minorities are more moral than majorities.

However, the problem is bigger than reporting political news. Correct, unbiased information is essential in any democratic country. Most media outlets, particularly newspapers, are owned by wealthy, powerful individuals who influence editorial opinion. Conrad Black's authority in this regard has been well established. He was quoted in the *Globe and Mail* on May 28, 1998, "We own slightly over 40 percent of this country's daily newspaper circulation, which hardly constitutes a monopoly."

If anyone can exercise monopolistic control over an information resource we should be concerned. Undoubtedly there is an increasing concentration of media ownership in fewer hands. This, together with less money for public service broadcasting, the rampant commercialization of news and information and the commercial exploitation of the new communication technology, threatens to limit accountability, the diversity of views and the ability of citizens to obtain information needed to make informed decisions about political affairs.

There is no law to prevent Conrad Black or Can West Global from buying every newspaper and every radio and television station in Canada. Legislation must be formulated to curb any concentration of media ownership or to prevent broadcasters from owning newspapers. Our Competition Act is far too ineffective. Britain, Sweden, Italy, Germany and France all have developed better measures than Canada. We live in a capitalist system and therefore newspapers will be owned by capitalists. Last year the Canadian government announced that a committee will be set up to examine concentration of media ownership in Canada.

Television is often not helpful in conveying political news because, except for question period in the House of Commons, its format suggests that all any citizen needs to know about a political matter can be pictured in a minute and a half. Ratings are the essential part of any program including the news.

The media has a constitutionally affirmed freedom but it must not allow political programs or news which has unacknowledged bias, inaccuracy, conclusions contrived to mislead or neglect of facts essential to a realistic understanding. An example of this would be during the 1988 election when Brian Mulroney defeated John Turner for the second time. Well after the writ was dropped and the election campaign was underway, the *Globe and Mail* had a story that John Turner would resign and a new Liberal leader would take over. This was repeated solemnly on the CBC news by Peter Mansbridge. This ridiculous story was concocted by reporters who had not the slightest knowledge of political processes and what was involved in getting a new leader for any political party.

Many political journalists do not know Canadian history, polling methodology or understand any part of the country but their own.

The media loves to report political poll results because they give an instant story. Previous polls can be compared to the newest ones. Trends can be suggested. Prognostications can be made. The political news story virtually writes itself and it also conveys the aura of scientific analysis and allows reporters to become political experts. Let us look at how polls work.

Pollsters put their questions to a selection of persons drawn from a larger population. They sample the opinions of a small group to get a sense of what the larger group thinks, just as a cook might sample a spoonful of soup to find out how the whole pot is going to taste. While no sample can be guaranteed to exactly match the larger population there are statistical methods to determine how close the results may be.

Say the sample size is 1600 persons. If the individuals are truly drawn at random, 19 times out of 20 the result you get for all 1600 respondents won't be off by more than 2.5 percentage points—plus or minus—from the result if you could poll the entire population. So if the poll states 40 percent of the people contacted would vote for Party X if an election were held today, the number of Party X supporters in the whole country might be as high as 42.5 percent or as low as 37.5 percent. That is going to happen 19 times out of 20 which means that one poll in every 20 could be a "rogue poll"—one whose numbers don't fall within the expected margin of error. Commonsense indicates the more people you interview the more accurate your poll.

There is certainly no question that polling is a permanent part of our democratic system and greatly influences voters in an election. As pollster Martin Goldfarb says,

"Polling today is to the politician and policymaker what the stock market is to the financial analyst."

But polls have many flaws. They claim to have scientific precision and most people tend to accept their findings uncritically. Computer printouts of poll results lead us to believe they are a sort of infallible truth. The methodology of polls and the influences of them indicate that they are replacing ideas and commonsense as the gods of politics.

Parliamentary democracy means we elect MPs or MLAs to lead, to take risks, to stand for something more than the latest quasi-collective public wisdom or the latest quasi-popular feeling, which may be based on emotion or ignorance. Free trade was a case in point. Polls on this complicated issue measured the views of people who frequently had no idea what the subject meant and, until they were asked, rarely thought about it. The assumption by pollsters that they were obtaining the opinion of an informed public on this matter was clearly not correct.

Pollsters pretend that polls are not different during or between elections. The question: "If a Canadian federal election were held today which party would you vote for?" is flawed because respondents are often not aware of platforms, candidates or leaders.

Modern technology such as answering machines in many homes also interferes with accuracy although the pollsters seldom admit it. You will not find a poll statistic indicating the times a call did not reach an individual or family. In an age of answering machines and call display, finding randomly selected people has become much harder. Pollsters say they have to dial five phone numbers to complete one interview. About half of those they reach hang up or refuse to take part. In wealthier areas many residences have unlisted numbers.

In an article in the *Vancouver Sun* on the federal 2000 election, Eric Vanderham, president of C. V. Marketing Research, said as election polls become frequent, more people are refusing to talk to pollsters. "People are getting bombarded by it," the pollster told the Canadian Public Relations Society on November 17, 2000. He informed reporters following the speech that increasingly high refusal rates raises questions about the accuracy of the polls. "Refusal rates can be 20, 30, 40, 50 percent," he said. And as the refusal rate goes up, the chance that the poll represents a true random sample goes down.

Polls cannot indicate respondents who will not bother to vote on election day. In the 1997 federal election, only 67 percent of eligible Canadian voters cast ballots. In 2000 it was 60.5 percent. Of the hundreds of political polls taken before each of these elections over 33 percent of the people gave insignificant answers, because they did not vote.

Government by public opinion polls is not more democratic. If a Canadian citizen gives his views at a meeting or gathering he must be prepared to defend his opinion. The anonymity of a poll means that a citizen has no involvement and thus can base his viewpoint on a whim. Polls thus trivialize public opinion.

Nevertheless polling numbers of people, done properly, can be a measure of a larger population better than any other method we have. The emphasis must be placed on "done properly."

History shows that polls are often done improperly. Gallup was the first pollster to recognize the value of the publicity that numbers could generate. But Gallup, in the 1948 US presidential election, along with major pollsters Crossley and Roper, all had Dewey beating Truman. Gallup, also, in the 1957 Canadian election had the Liberals winning easily but the voters gave John Diefenbaker's Tories a minority government.

Theodore White's account of the 1960 US election in *The Making of the President* greatly influenced polling in Canada. By the Trudeau era, polling was a permanent and increasingly costly procedure in politics. In the 1980s and up to today polling has become epidemic. Democracy itself is undermined by the influence of polls and pollsters who often seem to replace elected representatives as determinants of political action. Today polling is a 300 to 400 million dollar industry in Canada each year. Because of the large sums of money involved, pollsters sometimes arrange questions to suit the ideas of persons who pay for polls. Results that mesh exactly with the pre-survey desires of clients come up frequently. More than half of the major polling companies are attached either to a political party or media outlet.

On November 17, 2000, the *Vancouver Sun* published poll results of the major companies in connection with the federal election held on November 27, 2000. The actual results of the election are added plus 1997 and 1993 outcomes. It should be noted that author Claire Hoy says anybody can predict the outcome of any election just by repeating the popular vote percent of the previous election and be within an acceptable margin of error most of the time. A comparison of the 1993, 1997 and 2000 elections show that this is true.

Survey period	Release date	Liberal	Alliance	Bloc	PC	NDP	Undecided	No. polled	% error
Compass Nov 11-14	Nov 16	45	25	10	10	8	19	1,275	2.8
Ipsos-Reid Nov 10-11	Nov 12	40	28	11	9	9	n/a	1,050	3.0
Compass Nov 9-10	Nov 11	43	24	12	8	8	18	1,600	2.5
Environics Oct 31-Nov 6	Nov 8	48	26	9	8	8	19	1,857	2,3
Ipsos-Reid Oct 27-Nov 1	Nov 2	42	29	10	8	9	7	2,500	2.0
Environics Oct 26-30	Nov 2	45	29	11	7	7	19	1,339	2.7
EKOS Research Oct 23-26	Oct 27	47.1	27.9	9.2	8.1	7	13.6	2,265	2.1
Decima Research Oct 17-26	Oct 27	44.3	24	8.5	9.5	9.9	14.1	2,000	2.19
Ipsos-Reid Oct 19-25	Oct 26	45	28	9	8	8	n/a	1,500	2.5
Leger Marketing Oct 15-22	Oct 25	48	21	10	10	10	6	1,503	2.1
Nov 27 2000 Election % of popular vote seats		41 173	26 66	11 37	12 12	9 13			
1997 Election % of popular vote seats		38 155	19 60	11 44	19 20	11 21			
1993 Election % of popular vote seats		41 177	19 52	14 54	16 2	7 9			

As the reader can see, the popular vote does not necessarily translate into seats. For example, in 1993 the Conservatives had 16 percent of the popular vote which only gave them two seats. After every provincial and federal election there are letters to the editor condemning our "rotten" electoral system and recommending preferential voting. This was dealt with in Chapter 2.

How, then, do we determine if a political poll has been done properly? Fortunately the federal Elections Act sets out some criteria in Bill C-2 which was passed on May 31, 2000. These rules apply only during the 36 days before the actual vote.

> 3.27. *The first person who transmits the results of an election survey that is not based on recognized statistical methods to the public during an election period and any person who transmits within 24 hours after they are first transmitted to the public must indicate that the survey was not based on recognized statistical methods.*
> 3.26. (1) *The first person who transmits the results of an election survey—other than a survey that is described in section 3.27—to the public during an election period and any person who transmits them to the public within 24 hours after they are first transmitted to the public must provide the following together with the results:*
> (a) *the name of the sponsor of the survey;*
> (b) *the name of the person or organization that conducted the survey;*
> (c) *the date on which or the period during which the survey was conducted;*
> (d) *the population from which the sample of respondents was drawn;*

(e) the number of people who were contacted to participate in the survey; and

(f) if applicable, the margin of error in respect of the data obtained.

(2) In addition to the information referred to in subsection (1) the following must be provided in the case of the transmission to the public by means other than broadcasting:

(a) the wording of the survey questions in respect of which data is obtained; and

(b) the means by which a report referred to in subsection (3) may be obtained.

(3) A sponsor of an election survey shall, at any time during an election period after the results of the survey are transmitted to the public, provide, on request, a copy of a written report on the results of the survey, as transmitted in subsection (1). The report shall include the following, as applicable:

(a) the name of the sponsor of the survey;

(b) the name of the person or organization that conducted the survey;

(c) the date on which or the period during which the survey was conducted;

(d) information about the method used to collect the data from which the survey results are derived, including

(i) the sampling method,

(ii) the population from which the sample was drawn

(iii) the size of the initial sample

(iv) the number of individuals who were asked to participate in the survey and the numbers and respective percentages of them who participated in the *survey, refused to participate in the survey, and were ineligible to participate in the survey,*

(v) the dates and time of day of the interviews,

(vi) the method used to recalculate date to take into account in the survey the results of participants who expressed no opinion, were undecided or failed to respond to any or all of the survey questions, and

(vii) any weighting factors or normalization procedures used in deriving the results of the survey; and

(e) the wording of the survey questions and, if applicable, the margins of error in respect of the data obtained.

How many election opinion polls has the reader seen which contained all of the above? Probably none. A typical report of a poll goes as follows:

"The latest Angus Reid poll shows Liberals with 43 percent support, the Alliance with 25 percent and the Tories well back with 10—the lowest point in their history." (*The Vancouver Sun*, August 2000).

There is no date of the poll, no question sample, no data on the number of respondents or where they live, no name of the party who hired Angus Reid for the poll or the method of sampling, and no margin of error.

Let us examine each of the sections of the federal Election Act:

a) "the name of the sponsor of the survey."
This is important because all poll results which indicate

they were paid for by political operatives are suspect. For many years those polls were often not designed to be helpful but were partisan while maintaining anonymity. Who pays for the polls is of crucial importance. In cases involving anonymous payments, ethics is sometimes not as important as effect.

b) "the name of the person or organization that conducted the survey."

The reputation of the pollster doing the survey often determines how significant the results are. Anyone can say, "I'm a pollster," when he or she may have little expertise to do the task. There are no standards even though in Canada the Professional Market Research Society and the Canadian Association of Market Research Organizations promote non-binding guidelines.

Pollsters hired by political parties sometimes enjoy genius status: Martin Goldfarb when Trudeau was Prime Minister, Allan Gregg who worked for Joe Clark and later when he joined Decima Research. Also, George Gallup, who had the first major polling organization. The latter has usually been hired by politicians even when his polls have fluctuated wildly from time to time.

Recently the Angus Reid Group, Canada's leading pollster, has been acquired by Ipsos, a Paris-based company. Other Canadian pollsters include Michael Adam of Environics Research Group, Michael Marzolini of Pollara, John Mykytyshyn of Canadian Voter Contact and Frank Graves of Ekes Research Associates.

c) "the date on which or the period during which the survey was conducted."

This prevents older survey results from being presented as new.

d) "the population from which the sample of respondents was drawn."

In a federal election a national poll must cover every province and territory if the question asks, "What political party will you vote for?" The survey must include rural areas, urban areas and remote areas to make the results "scientific."

e) "the number of people who were contacted to participate in the survey."

In a national poll, the opinion of 1600 Canadians out of 30 million means very little but pollsters may claim that their poll was conducted among a representative cross-section with scientific accuracy.

In many cases a large percentage of respondents answer questions by saying they "don't know" or are "undecided" or they "won't say." It is not unusual in an election period for 20, 30 or over 40 percent of the sample to make such a reply. Yet Gallup, Angus Reid and most other major pollsters round up the total in published figures to 100 percent as though everyone had given a specific reply.

f) "if applicable, the margin of error in respect to the date obtained"

The "if applicable" should be eliminated because the margin of error should always be provided as a rough measure of accuracy. This really means that the pollsters should explain how they arrived at the figures they show.

In the June 1993 federal election during the month of March previous to the writ being dropped, four polls were conducted by Angus Reid, Gallup and Environics and Camquest. Their survey predicted:

1. A Tory sweep: The Gallup survey conducted between March 25 and April 12 gave the Kim Campbell-led Conservatives 50 percent of the voter support with the Liberals trailing badly at 29 percent. (In the election the Conservatives obtained 16 percent.)
2. A Tory majority: Both Comquest and Reid, in surveys conducted March 8–15 and March 15–18 respectively, said the Tories would win a majority under Campbell. Comquest had the party winning 45 to 32 percent over the Liberals; Reid by 43 to 25 percent. (In the election the Conservatives got 41 percent.)
3. A Liberal minority: Environics predicted in a survey taken from March 10 to March 25 that Jean Chretien's Liberals would outvote the Tories by 36 to 33 percent.

Environics went to 2000 voters, Reid to 1500, Comquest to 1440 and Gallup to 1000. All four pollsters claimed an accuracy or margin of error of between 2.5 percent and 3.1 percent, 19 times out of 20.

The margins of error were supposed to provide us with an evaluation of the accuracy of the sample. In these polls they did not. Let us see how margins of error are produced.

The calculations involve statistics related to the bell-shaped curve. The lower the margin of error the more accurately the views of those surveyed matches those of the entire population. If 1600 respondents were questioned the margin of error would be the square root of 1600 (40) divided into 100 which would give 2.5. If only 400 were asked it would be 20 divided into 100 giving a reliability rate of 5.0. So if a pollster is willing to accept a higher margin of error, he or she can reduce the size of the sample.

The Elections Act also asks for a written report, on request, which covers such things as the time of day of the interview, the wording of the survey questions, the number of persons who refused to participate in the survey and the method of sampling.

The main thrust of all polling is that the sampling is done randomly. This usually means taking census enumeration areas and selecting a proportionate number of households from each area. Then a computer dials random phone numbers. When polls have to be done in two or three days, pollsters will often not make call backs when they should make four call backs on four consecutive days before choosing another name in order to keep the sample's randomness as pure as possible.

Obviously the size of the sample is crucial. National surveys cost $50 to $60 per person so many pollsters try to cut corners. This means that so-called "scientific" sampling can yield unscientific results.

Every time a pollster deviates from his overall sample into a sub-sample of any kind the margin of error increases. If a national poll breaks down voting preferences into provincial units in say, Manitoba, where a national survey might mean that only about 54 Manitobans were asked. The margin of error for that result would be 18, plus or minus. Therefore if it had the Canadian Alliance at 40 they could be anywhere from 22 to 58 percent.

How many times have we heard commercials in which claims such as "four out of five doctors recommend" are made? The sample might consist of a total of five doctors of which four favoured the product and also happened to be stockholders of that company.

The wording of the survey question is another important aspect of polling. Semantics or words and their meanings is significant. The question "Do you own a car?" has many implications. What does "you" mean? What if the wife answers the question but the car is registered in her husband's name. What does "own" mean? Does a leased car count? What does "car" mean? Does a van or four-wheel drive vehicle count?

If the question is "Which party's candidate do you think you would favour?" it will not be the same as "Which party would you be most likely to support?" The difference between being asked about a "party" and being asked about a "party's candidate" could be significant.

The question is sometimes phrased so that only a glib answer is required. For example:

Should the Prime Minister seek a fourth term of office?" "Should Joe Clark continue as leader of the Conservative Party?"

Special interest groups often structure poll questions to obtain a particular result and then claim the public supports them. Full disclosure of details of polling would help deflect the influence of unscientific procedures. Newspapers, television and radio outlets should be required to include methodological details of polls, particularly on the number of respondents.

Every poll is a snapshot of a moment in time—of an object in motion and by that definition is changing even as it is being taken. We become spellbound by numbers and when pollsters talk about a margin of error of 4.1 plus or minus we tend to think that it has the same precision as a tool-and-die maker casting a die. Actually the margin of error is based on a perfect poll which does not exist.

In full page newspaper ads in September, well before the 2000 federal election, Elections Canada gave the following information on opinion surveys which would be in effect during the 36-day election period.

> *"Anyone who first releases the results of an election opinion survey during an election must state who sponsored the survey, who conducted it, when and how the sample was drawn, how many people participated and the margin of error.*
> *Non-broadcasters (e.g. newspapers, Internet sites) must publish the wording of the questions and where a copy of the survey may be obtained.*
> *Anyone else who publishes the results within 24 hours of the first publication must provide the same information."*

Nearly every day following the commencement of the 2000 federal election a fresh poll was announced—over television, radio broadcasts, in magazines and in newspapers. Not one followed the regulations which had been so widely advertised by Elections Canada.

Inquiries by the author to Elections Canada regarding survey violations were met with statements to the effect that a citizen must send a complaint in writing to the Commissioner in charge, Raymond Landry, who would then investigate it. However, Section 151 of the Elections Act states that the Commissioner may take action himself if he feels it is in the public interest.

"Section 151. If the Commissioner believes on reasonable grounds that an offence under this Act has been committed and is of the view that the public interest justifies it, the Commissioner may institute or cause to be instituted a prosecution for the offence.

a) after an inquiry under section 510; or
b) where no inquiry has been held, on the Commissioner's own initiative, or after the receipt, within six months after its commission, of a written complaint alleging the commission of the offence."

The author sent a written complaint to the Commissioner of Canada Elections on November 20, 2000. Nine months later Mr. Landry replied in a letter dated August 27, 2001. He wrote that because of "the evidential and other difficulties of instituting a prosecution, we have decided that it would not be in the public interest to proceed with a prosecution."

The obtuseness illustrated by this civil servant's letter shows how fearful and ineffective the Commissioner's office is in prosecuting powerful media management like Hollinger or Can West Global. Obviously, many published election survey results violated the Act but as the legislation was new, Mr. Landry's lawyers did not know how to handle it or were fearful of media repercussions. Jean-Pierre Kinglsey, the C.E.O. of Elections Canada must certainly have been aware of what was going on.

Before the next federal election this situation must be remedied and penalties publicized. Surely the lawyers employed by Elections Canada can make a case for requiring the news media to conform to the Elections Act.

It is evident that the federal election of November 27,

2000 had poll results announced in exactly the same manner as they had been in the elections of 1997 and 1993.

It is suggested, too, that the total cost of each poll should be published so that the public knows how much was spent. This knowledge would help to rate pollsters and possibly get rid of those who are incompetent. Generally the more costly the poll, the more "scientific" it will be.

The emergence of new political parties like the Canadian Alliance not only expands the choices for voters but also involves outcomes more difficult for the polls to predict. Small swings in popular support can thus produce large shifts in the distribution of seats.

Unfortunately, as for listing the five major political parties, many Canadians can't even name them let alone tell you anything about them.

In the towns and villages of nineteenth century Canada, politics was personal, social and almost entirely oral. Political meetings, mass rallies, parades, debates and discussions involved most people of a community. There were few distractions like sports, movies, radio, television or computers. The rise of daily newspapers, magazines, radio and television stations and the internet has changed the playing field. Talking and listening to a large number of people, particularly in urban ridings, has become almost impossible.

This writer can remember elections decades ago when most candidates depended on their supporters to come to a central place and go over cards of electors. In each case the political support was written on the cards if it were known. On election day all the voters on the party's cards would be phoned and transportation would be provided if needed.

Canadian political parties and candidates now depend on hired experts: campaign managers, advertising agencies, writers, television directors, researchers, media advisors, ubiquitous pollsters and phone banks.

For the last fifty years the media and polls have significantly affected elections. Let us take advantage of this by providing "free-time" political broadcasting on both T.V. and radio. Stations would be compensated from the public treasury. Programming would, of course, be given in the same format on English and French stations. In the same fashion, national or provincial print advertising of page ads would be paid for by the taxpayer.

Why not also have scientific political polls done by a non-partisan organization paid for by taxpayers? If this could be worked out it would require less money for each political party to run campaigns.

The next logical step would be to prohibit political contributions from sources other than individual Canadian citizens. Once business, advocacy group and union funding of politics were eliminated there would be more public confidence in politics. In addition, funding of polls should count as an election expense.

What we must avoid at all costs is government by polls. The latter must never supplant the wisdom of the statesman. Polls can remove any principle, direction or philosophy required to guide a country as the development of policies gives way to a development of strategies.

There are five major reasons why political opinion polls should be prohibited a week before election day in spite of this possibly violating the Charter of Rights and Freedoms:

1. Polls unduly influence elections.
2. Polls invade the privacy of citizens.
3. Polls oversimplify the issues and trivialize opinions.

4. Polls are often unreliable.
5. Polls do not meet the requirements of the Elections Act.

In a perfect society there would be properly conducted polls reported by a responsible and knowledgeable media. This is a procedure devoutly to be wished but until that time comes public opinion polls are blunt instruments of prediction and are susceptible to many forms of error, inadvertent or contrived. Poll statistics are often used by groups who wish to oppose a government policy.

Another problem of political polls is personnel, which is partly but not entirely a matter of money. A reliable survey requires the services of good statisticians, good psychologists and good interviewers, to mention a few. The first two are expensive and the last have to be numerous so it is often difficult to give them as much screening and training as they should have. Some pollsters have been able to survive in spite of personnel deficiencies because most politicians and media people, once sold on the idea of conducting a poll, will underestimate the importance of finding a qualified pollster to carry it off.

The usefulness of opinion polls is no longer in question, but it still pays to view their results with intelligent and educated skepticism.

On May 16, 2001, in a provincial election, British Columbians gave the Liberals 57 percent of the vote, the NDP 22 and the Green Party 12. But throughout the campaign, polls pegged NDP support at no higher than 17 percent of decided voters. The Liberals were never lower in the polls than 61 percent and the Greens were often in a statistical deadlock with the NDP.

CHAPTER EIGHT
Our House of Commons, Our Legislatures and Our Political Parties

> "Man's capacity for justice makes democracy possible but man's inclination to injustice makes democracy necessary."
> —Reinold Niebuhr (American theologian)

The House of Commons and the provincial legislatures derive their respective powers from Section 91 to 95 of the Constitution Act, 1867, formerly known as the British North American Act.

Section 91 deals with the powers of the national parliament. It begins, "It shall be lawful for the Queen, by and with the Advice and Consent of the Senate and House of Commons, to make Laws for the Peace, Order, and good Government of Canada, in relation to all matters not coming within the Classes of Subjects by this Act assigned exclusively in the Legislatures of the Provinces...." It is then asserted that for the sake of "greater Certainty" various "Classes of Subjects" which fall under the federal parliament's legislative authority will be specified. Among these one finds headings such as (91.2) "The Regulation of Trade and Commerce," (91.3) "The raising of Money by any mode or System of Taxation," (91.7) "Militia, Military and Naval Service, and Defence," (91.24) "Indians and Lands reserved for the Indians," and (91.27) "The Criminal Law, except the Constitution of Courts of Criminal Jurisdiction, but including the Procedure in Criminal Matters."

Section 92 includes those matters which the legislatures of each province "may exclusively make Laws in relation to . . . ." Among this list are (92.2) "Direct Taxation within the Province in order to the raising of a Revenue for Provincial Purposes," (92.5) "The Management and Sale of the Public Lands belonging to the Province and of the Timber and Wood thereon," (92.7) "The Establishment, Maintenance, and Management of Hospitals, Asylums, Charities, and Eleemosynary [charitable] Institutions in and for the Province, other than Marine Hospitals," (92.8) "Municipal Institutions in the Province," (92.13) "Property and Civil Rights in the Province," and (92.14) "The Administration of Justice in the Province, including the Constitution, Maintenance, and Organization of Provincial Courts, both of Civil and Criminal jurisdiction, and including Procedure in Civil Matters in those Courts." The provincial level of government has authority over municipal or local governments. These local units thus derive their authority from another, more senior level of government.

Section 93 awards responsibility over education to the provincial legislatures subject to allowances for then existing denominational school systems while 94 recognizes the federal parliament's ability to work for legislative uniformity among the provinces. Section 95 recognizes that both levels of government would share authority (concurrent powers) over agriculture and immigration. Provincial legislation on these matters can not be contrary to acts of the federal parliament.

In Canada's federation, one level may not do away with, or substantially alter the authority of the other without joint agreements. These efforts have been mostly unsuccessful. Attempts to change complex issues like debt reduction, transfer payments to provinces, Quebec sovereignty, aboriginal grievances, Senate reform, etc. have largely resulted in failure. Witness Meech Lake (1987–90), the Charlottetown referendum (1992) and the Quebec referendums.

On a more positive side, first ministers' conferences and meetings of federal and provincial ministers have become a benchmark of Canadian intergovernmental relations. These must continue.

Parliamentary democracy is adversarial and this is even reflected in the design of the building where it meets. Government and opposition face one another across an area which separates them by the length of two swords. Those who wish to do away with political parties should realize that this adversarial aspect of the House of Commons and the provincial legislatures shapes their basic operating rules and procedures which are enforced by the Speaker who is supposed to be neutral.

Because of this and a host of other reasons, parties remain necessary. They could well relax their iron grip on their MPs and all parties should work to create more opportunities for free votes as long as that doesn't raise a question of confidence in the government. Free votes on abortion or capital punishment are examples of how the House of Commons can work. The last free vote occurred on June 8, 1999 when the House of Commons ruled on a motion stating that marriage is and should be the union of one man and one woman, to the exclusion of all others. This definition of marriage was supported by a vote of 216 to 55.

MPs and MLAs must also be given a better chance to make their own bills into laws. Private members' bills are usually "talked out" (no vote is taken before the allotted time expires) or defeated. The "talking out" provision should be abolished and each bill put to a vote.

It is evident, too, that the party system often results in backbench MPs or MLAs playing a minor role. A political answer is to make all party parliamentary committees more powerful and independent, letting them take an active and less partisan role in studying and recommending amendments to government initiatives before they become embedded in law. To enable committees to become more effective, chairmen should get supplementary salaries and both chairs and committee members should remain in their posts for several years. This would increase their expertise and give them more credibility.

At the federal level parliamentary committees should be able to scrutinize spending decisions and make appointments of the privacy and access-to-information commissioner, the auditory general and the ethics counsellor. The latter should report directly to the House of Commons, not the prime minister.

However, the Canadian parliamentary system requires party loyalty and the realization that Canada is better off with MPS or MLAs in a party than it would be under any alternative arrangement. Their regional or personal views must often give way to larger policy and the national or provincial interest. It is acknowledged that party discipline is not understood or appreciated by many Canadian citizens. Cabinet government rests upon party discipline to control the legislative agenda.

It should be noted that the forty minute oral "Question Period" in the Canadian House of Commons is unique in that nowhere else in the world is the central government held to daily account by being subjected to questions on its programs or policies.

Party discipline implies a negative constraint on parliamentary behaviour. But nearly all MPs and MLAs realize that the disadvantages are outweighed by the advantages. In the Reform Party's (not the Canadian Alliance) Statement of Principles, number 15 says "We believe in the accountability of elected representatives to the people who elect them, and that the duty of elected members to their constituents should supercede their obligations to their political parties."

This is naïve because of the difficulty in ascertaining the wishes of about 100,000 people in each federal riding and roughly 60,000 provincially. It would result in a weakening of all political parties in the operation of the House of Commons or the legislatures if this principal was adopted.

In addition it is necessary that the House of Commons and the provincial legislatures should have a fixed term of four years. The present system whereby the Prime Minister or the premiers can call elections when they wish, usually for tactical reasons, is an undemocratic provision and must be changed to a specific fixed election date on a four-year cycle.

Are political parties vital then to our Canadian democracy? The answer is a resounding yes. Citizens should work for something that is larger than themselves.

The kind of parties that have grown up in Canada are coalitions of regional, economic and ideological interests. These parties-within-parties vie with one another for influence over the general party policy. That policy is a synthesis of the internal competing interests, filtered through the judgment of the party leadership. Leaders should take close account of the disparate views within their parties. If they ignore too many of them too often, they may find themselves out of jobs. Stockwell Day is an example.

Once a policy has been formulated, the party's elected members in parliament or the provincial assemblies are expected to support it, along with the policies made extemporaneously by the leadership and party caucus. The argument is frequently put that this makes eunuchs of individual members; but the alternative would be to make a eunuch of parliament. If every member were free to make his or her own individual policy, it would be a Tower of Babel in which little worthwhile would ever be accomplished. Much the same would be true if there were a multiplicity of small parties, each pursuing its own particular interest. The Fourth Republic of France, which saw 24 governments between 1946 and 1958, is a case in point.

"Party divisions, whether on the whole operating for good or evil, are things inseparable from free government," Edmund Burke wrote. This is evident wherever governments are *not* free. Dictators have always provided the best advertisements for the party system through the fear they show of it. "We abhor political parties. We are against political parties. We have none," General Francisco Franco of Spain once said.

An effective opposition—effective tactically, though it may be weak numerically—is essential to good government.

If nothing else, it tends to keep the ruling party on the straight and narrow. "Given a government with a big surplus, a big majority, and a weak opposition, you could debauch a committee of archangels," Sir John A. Macdonald once remarked.

Though it is a human institution reflecting all the imperfections of the human race, a parliamentary system made up of competing parties is well-designed to meet Jeremy Bentham's primary aim of government: "The greatest good of the greatest number." Yet when we look around us today, we see the system being treated with either unconscious or open disdain. This is manifest in the trend in recent years to launch political action outside the established process, by demonstrations, boycotts, illegal strikes, and outright terrorism. It is a product of the "instant age"—an age of instant food, instant entertainment, instant gratification of all manner of desires. Protest groups of visible minorities, homosexuals, anti-abortionists, etc. have direct participation and television publicity.

Political action within the system may come slower, but it is surer and fairer to all sections of our society. It would be more democratic for activists to take their causes to the grass roots level of party politics, which extends "power to the people" in an orderly fashion. It would not, admittedly, be as exciting or as much fun as shouting slogans and waving placards. The democratic process demands patience, tolerance, and realism from those who participate in it.

It is tragic that fewer than five percent of Canadians contribute to the finances of a political party especially as these political donations may be deducted in part from the contributor's income tax.

We find that in the past most political parties operated both at the federal and provincial levels. However, in the 1990s, two of the five parties represented in the House of Commons did not have provincial branches and two did not contest federal elections. This separation of federal and provincial politics plus a proliferation of splinter parties means that there are more divisions in the country as parties are agents of integration in Canada's highly diverse society.

Adding to this we find increasing numbers involved in single issues which seem manageable or comprehensible. This gives rise to "interest" groups in health care, education, crime, trade issues or the environment. Also we have "rights" movements in areas such as gender, ethnicity, racial identity or abortion. These "rights" groups often divide Canadians into antagonistic groups.

Only a few times in the twentieth century has a winning party in a federal election won more than half of the popular vote. This trend will continue as more parties contest elections and the chances of minority governments with consequent political instability and frequent elections will increase.

Minority governments are often unable to respond quickly and decisively to challenges, particularly if the business cycle brings a recession.

In addition to the major parties—Liberals, Canadian Alliance, NDP, Conservatives and the Bloc—there were a number of fringe parties in the 2000 federal election: Christian Heritage, Communist, Western, Green, Libertarian, Rhinoceros, Action, Commonwealth, Marijuana, Reform, Social Credit, Canada, Renewal, Marxist-Leninist, National, Natural Law, Option, Nationaliste, Populist and Monetary

Law. Imagine if ten of these parties with an equal number of MPs tried to govern Canada. At the provincial level, there were 36 registered political parties in British Columbia fighting the election of May 16, 2001.

In spite of this, government is, as has been said, more effective and responsible because of political parties. Ideally a political party is a team of individuals attempting to achieve a collective approach to political issues. Political parties are advocates of differing social and economic legislation and thus give citizens choices for the latter's vote.

An argument against political parties is that respect for them is in many instances low. Election promises are frequently broken or changed. Sometimes this happens because finances are worse than the elected party realized. Often circumstances change and so election platforms change when a party gains power. It is wrong to assume that when a party receives a mandate to govern it means that it loses its mandate if it deviates from election pledges. The mandate is to deal with any issue that comes up during the life of that government. This is true whether the government party receives the majority of the popular vote or not.

Political parties recruit the political policy-makers and decision-makers in Canada. Parties also ensure that the MLAs or MPs have a loyalty to the organization that got them elected.

Not only do these parties provide candidates but they also help the public to understand their programs and so Canadians may use politics as symbols to which they can attach allegiance.

In short, political parties are essential to our Canadian democracy.

CHAPTER NINE
Our Democratic Future

"Democracy is not a short-term goal and not just a flag to be waved by one country: it is the long-term hope of the entire human species."
—Louis Dudak (Canadian aphorist)

Subtitles of this book could be "Looking for a better democracy" or "Democratizing democracy." It is hoped that *Improving Canada's Democracy* does more than shed light on several democratic strands in the web of human experience but that it has provided specific ideas for a stronger web in our entire Canadian democracy.

These concepts included major reforms in education, voting, the Senate, patronage, the provincial legislatures, the House of Commons, political parties, news media, political polls and federal representation.

Democracy at the municipal or city level is reasonably satisfactory because it is closer to the people who are served by it. Most urban dwellers have seen members of their council at civic events and council meetings are also easier to attend than provincial legislatures or the House of Commons.

Nevertheless, two concerns are occurring in municipal

politics. The first is the amalgamation of municipalities in so-called megacities. Halifax in 1996, Toronto in 1998, Ottawa in 2000 and Montreal in 2002 are examples. These amalgamations mean that over 400 Canadian municipalities will lose their political identities. Municipalities don't have to amalgamate but they have to co-operate in big ticket areas like transit, roads, water, pollution and sewers.

The second is the growing power of regional district bodies whose members are unelected. In British Columbia the largest group is the Greater Vancouver Regional District where tiny villages have representation which is grossly out of proportion to their population. Examples are Lions Bay's 1,350 residents with the same vote on the GVRD board as Port Moody's 25,000 or by each 100,000 citizens in Vancouver. This situation must be corrected and members elected by voters in equal population representation.

There are, of course, other Canadian democratic problems that need to be addressed but will be partially resolved by a better democracy. The matter of regional alienation, especially in Quebec and the West, and the settlement of aboriginal land claims to name only two significant ones. Let us always remember, however, that there is a lot more that unites Canada than divides it.

Leadership races should be governed by rules of disclosure passed by parliament or the legislatures. This disclosure legislation must have teeth to penalize any party who bends or breaks them. As it stands now a leadership campaign can cost a party more than an election.

Major democratic constitutional reforms must be

brought about by national referendums. In the past there has been a reluctance to improve our democracy by submitting constitutional amendments to the people. This must be carried out more frequently in this century in order to bring about an improved democratic system.

But it is more than making democratic constitutional changes. Efforts to improve our democracy means a life-long commitment by citizens. Democracy is a sacred trust and represents values that are within each of us. Mel Hurtig said in 1992, "Political reform should be at the top of our national agenda, right next to the economy. Yet, somehow, the Conservatives, Liberals and New Democrats seem to have almost totally forgotten the issue."

The court of public opinion should insist on a more democratic vision and no less than a consecration to democracy is required. Every person is needed in the never-ending task of changing our democratic country for the better. Our true destiny in the twenty-first century is to become a leading democracy in the world.

The citizens of Canada will not only endure they will prevail. They have a spirit capable of compassion, sacrifice and fairness and Canadian democracy will enable us to meet the future with courage and honour and hope and pride which has often been the Canadian glory of the past. It is the betterment of our democratic society which is at stake. What is needed is a democratic purpose, a democratic goal in a new quest towards a democratic renewal in which all Canadians will benefit. Building an improved Canadian democracy, a democracy that enhances the rights of our citizens, is a great goal we can share as Canadians which will make Canada a stronger, better and more united country.

References

Archer, Keith, Gibbins, Roger, Knopff, Rainer, and Pal, Leslie. *Parameters of power*. Nelson, Toronto, 1995.

Armstrong, Joe. *Farewell the peaceful kingdom*. Stoddart Publishing, Toronto, 1995.

Bain, George. *Gotcha! How the media distort the news*. Key Porter Books Ltd., Toronto, 1994.

Barlow, Maude. *The fight of my life*. HarperCollins, Toronto, 1998.

Barlow, Maude and Winter, James. *The big black book*. Stoddart Publishing, Toronto, 1997.

Behiels, Michael, ed., *The Meech Lake primer*. University of Ottawa, Ottawa, 1989.

Bejermi, John. *How parliament works*. Boreallis Press, Ottawa, 2000.

Berger, Thomas. *Fragile freedoms*. Clarke Irwin and Co., Vancouver, B.C., 1981.

Berton, Pierre. *Why we act like canadians*. McClelland and Stewart, Toronto, 1982.

Bill C-2. *An act respecting the election of members of the House of Commons*. Parliamentary Publications, Ottawa Assented to 31st May, 2000.

Black, Conrad. *A life in progress*. Key Porter Books, Toronto, 1993.

Blakeney, A., and Sandford, B. *Political management in Canada: conversations on statecraft*. Second edition, University of Toronto Press, Toronto, 1998.

Bolt, Clarence. *Does Canada matter?* Ronsdale Press, Vancouver, B.C., 1999.

REFERENCES

Boyer, Patrick. *Hands-on democracy*. Stoddart Publishing, Toronto, 1993.

Brooks, Stephen. *Canadian democracy*. McClelland and Stewart, Toronto, 1993.

Burgess, Michael, ed. *Canadian federalism past, present and future*. Leicester University Press, London, England, 1990.

Cameron, Steven. *On the take: crime, corruption and greed in the Mulroney Years*. Macfarlane, Walter and Ross, Toronto, 1994.

Cardin, Jean-François. *A history of the Canadian constitution*. Global Vision Publishing Company, Montreal, 1996.

Castonguay, Claude. *Representation in the federal parliament*. Elections Canada, Ottawa, 1993.

Chambers, Tom. *Canadian politics*. Thompson Educational Publishing, Toronto, 1996.

Clark, Joe. *A nation too good to lose*. Key Porter Books, Toronto, 1994.

Cohen, A., and Granastein, J. *Trudeau's shadow*. Random House, Toronto, 1998.

Colombo, John. *Famous lasting words*. Douglas and McIntyre, Vancouver, B.C., 2000.

Coyne, Deborah and Valpy, Michael. *To match a dream*. McClelland and Stewart, Toronto, 1998.

Davis, Jack. *Popular politics*. Friesen, Vancouver, B.C., 1984.

Delacourt, Susan. *United we fall*. Viking, Toronto, 1993.

Deverall, John and Vezina, Greg. *Democracy eh?* Davies Publishing, Outremont, Quebec, 1993.

Dion, Stéphane. *Straight talk*. McGill-Queen's University Press, Montreal, 1999.

REFERENCES

Dobbin, Murray. *The myth of the good corporate citizen.* Stoddart Publishing, Toronto, 1998.

Fife, Robert and Warren, John. *A capital scandal.* Key Porter Books, Toronto, 1991.

Forbes, H.D. ed. *Canadian political thought.* Oxford University Press, Toronto, 1979.

Fotheringham, Allan. *Birds of a feather.* Key Porter Books, Toronto, 1989.

Gibbons, R., and Laforest, G., eds. *Beyond the impasse toward reconciliation.* The Institute for Research on Public Policy, Ottawa, 1998.

Granatstein, Jack. *Who killed Canadian history?* Random House, Toronto, 1998.

Grossman, Lawrence. *The electronic republic.* Penguin Publishing, New York, New York, 1995.

Hoy, Claire. *Margin of error: pollsters and the manipulation of canadian politics.* Key Porter Books, Toronto, 1989.

Hoy, Claire. *Nice work: the continuing scandal of Canada's senate.* McClelland and Stewart, Toronto, 1999.

Hurley, James. *Amending Canada's constitution.* Ministry of Supply and Services, Ottawa, 1996.

Hurtig, Mel. *At twilight in the country.* Stoddart Publishing, Toronto, 1996.

Jackson, Robert and Atkinson, Michael. *The canadian legislative system.* Gage Publishing, Toronto, 1980.

Johnston, Donald, ed. *Pierre Trudeau speaks out on Meech Lake.* General Paperbacks, Toronto, 1990.

Kent, Tom. *Getting ready for 1999.* Institute for Research on Public Policy, Halifax, Nova Scotia, 1989.

Krause, R., and Wagenberg, R.H. *Canadian government and politics.* Copp Clarke, Toronto, 1995.

Lazar, Harvey. *Non-constitutional renewal.* Institute of

REFERENCES

Intergovernmental Relations, Ottawa, 1998.

Lynch, Charles. *A funny way to run a country*. Hurtig Publishers, Edmonton, Alberta, 1986.

Mahler, Gregory. *New dimensions of Canadian federalism*. Associated University Presses, Cranbury, New Jersey, 1987.

Mair, Rafe. *Rants, raves and recollections*. Whitecap Books, Vancouver, B.C., 2000.

Malcolm, Andrew. *The Canadians*. Fitzhenry and Whiteside, Markham, Ontario, 1985.

Mallory, J.R. *The structure of Canadian government*. Gage, Toronto, 1984.

Manning, Preston. *The new Canada*. Macmillan, Toronto, 1992.

McIntosh, David. *Ottawa unbuttoned*. Stoddart Publishing, Toronto, 1987.

McKenna, Marian, ed. *The Canadian and American constitutions in comparative prospective*. University of Calgary Press, Calgary, Alberta, 1993.

McMenemy, John. *The language of Canadian politics*. Wilfred Laurier University Press, Waterloo, Ontario, 1995.

Miller, John and Hurst, Donald. *Gaining power*. Academic Press, Don Mills, Ontario, 1979.

Milner, Henry, ed. *Making every vote count*. Broadview Press, Peterborough, Ontario, 1999.

Minister of Public Works and Government Services. *A history of the vote in Canada*. Canadian Government Publishing, Ottawa, 1997.

Monahan, Patrick. *Meech Lake, the inside story*. University of Toronto, Toronto, 1991.

Morton, D. And Weinfold, M. *Who speaks for Canada?*

REFERENCES

McClelland and Stewart, Toronto, 1998.

Mowers, Cleo, ed. *Towards a new liberalism*. Orca Press, Victoria, B.C. 1991.

Nevitte, N., Blais, A., Gidenqil, E., and Nadeau, R. *Unsteady state, the 1997 Canadian federal election*. Oxford University Press, Don Mills, Ontario, 2000.

Radwanski, George, and Luttrell, Julia. *The will of a nation*. Stoddart Publishing, Toronto, 1992.

Rebick, Judy. *Imagine democracy*. Stoddart Publishing Co., Toronto, 2000.

Robinson, Judith. *This is on the house*. McClelland and Stewart, Toronto, 1957.

Russell, Peter. *Constitutional odyssey*. University of Toronto Press, Toronto, 1999.

Savoie, Donald. *Governing from the centre*, University of Toronto Press, 1999.

Tindal, Richard. *A citizen's guide to government*. McGraw-Hill Ryerson, Toronto, 1997.

Tullock, Gordon. *The new federalist*. The Fraser Institute, Vancouver, B.C., 1994.

Van Loon, Richard, and Whittington, Michael. *The Canadian political system*. McGraw-Hill Ryerson, Toronto, 1981.

Weaver, Jefferson. *Conquering statistics*. Plenum Trade, New York, New York, 1997.

Westmacott, M. and Mellon, H., eds. *Challenges to Canadian federalism*. Prentice-Hall Canada, Scarborough, Ontario, 1998.

Weston, Greg. *Reign of error*. McGraw-Hill Ryerson, Scarborough, Ontario, 1988.

Zolf, Larry. *Survival of the fattest*. Key Porter Books, Toronto, 1984.

Index

A
Access to Information Commissioner, 62
Adam, Michael, 79
Advisory Council on the Status of Women, 62
Armstrong, Joe, 10
Atomic Energy of Canada Limited, 62
Auditor-General, 62

B
Bank of Canada, 62
Bentham, Jeremy, 36, 95
Beveridge, William, 9
Black, Conrad, 69
Bouchard, Lucien, 11
Bourassa, Robert, 49, 51
British North America Act, 47, 89
Brooks, Stephen, 47, 55
Burke, Edmund, 94

C
Campbell, Kim, 81
Campbell, Michael, 66
Camquest, 81
Canada Post, 62
Canadian Alliance, 86
Canadian Ports Corporation, 62
Canadian Radio-television and Telecommunications Commission, 62
Charlottetown Accord, 39, 53-55, 91

Charter of Rights and Freedoms, 25, 61
Chretien, Jean, 12, 39, 81
Citizenship Court, 62
Clark, Joe, 15, 83
Clarkson, Adrienne (Governor-General), 11, 18
Constitution Act (1867), 41, 89
Constitution Act (1982), 50, 89
Council of Canadians, 11

D
Dawson, McGregor, 41
Day, Stockwell, 94
Diefenbaker, John, 74
Dudak, Louis, 98
Duplessis, Maurice, 61

E
Earnscliffe, 16
Einstein, Albert, 65
Elections Canada, 85
Ethics Commissioner, 62
Export Development Corporation, 62

F
Fathers of Confederation, 43
Fotheringham, Alan, 68
Francis, Diane, 38
Franco, Francisco (General), 94
Free Trade, 72

INDEX

G
Gallup, George, 73, 74, 79, 80, 81
Goldfarb, Martin, 79
Governor of the Bank of Canada, 62
Granatstein, Jack, 14
Graves, Frank, 79
Greater Vancouver Regional District, 99
Green Party, 88
Gregg, Allan, 79
Gzowski, Peter, 67

H
House of Commons, 16, 21, 25, 26, 42, 43, 61, 63, 91, 92
Hoy, Claire, 41, 44, 74
Hurtig, Mel, 100

I
Immigration and Refugee Board, 62
International Joint Commission, 62

K
Kingsley, Jean-Pierre, 21, 25

L
Landry, Raymond, 85
Laurier House, 16
Laurier, Wilfred, 12, 16, 48
Lesage, Jean, 49
Levesque, René, 50
Lortie Commission on Electoral Reform, 32
Loyal, Serge, 11

M
Macdonald, John A., 16, 47, 95
MacKenzie-King, William, 16, 48
Mansbridge, Peter, 70
Marzolini, Michael, 79
McLaughlin, Audrey, 39
Meech Lake Accord, 51, 52, 91
Mulroney, Brian, 39, 51-53, 63, 70
Mykytyshyn, John, 79

N
National Art Centre, 62
National Capital Commission, 62
National Citizens Coalition, 11
National Energy Board, 62
National Library, 16
National Parole Board, 62
National Railway, 62
National Transportation Agency, 62
National War Memorial, 16
Niebuhr, Reinold, 89

O
Olympic Games, 13
Organization for Econonic Cooperation and Development, 19
Ottawa, 16
Owen, Stephen, 63

P
Plebiscites (see referendums)
Proportional representation, 30-33

R
Radler, David, 67

INDEX

Recall, 37
Referendums, 36-40, 50, 57
Reid, Angus, 78, 80, 81
Representation Act, 26, 27
Rideau Hall, 16

S
Saul, John, 11
Security Intelligence Review Committee, 62
Senate, 26, 41-46
St. Laurent, Louis, 12
Supreme Court of Canada, 16, 35, 43, 51, 61

T
Trudeau, Pierre, 12, 14, 43, 49, 50, 54, 58, 60, 63, 74
Turner, John, 70

V
Vancouver Sun, 10, 11, 66, 73, 74, 78
Vanderham, Eric, 73
Via Rail, 62

W
White, Theodore, 74

Y
Yaffe, Barbara, 10

Z
Zolt, Larry, 41

ISBN 1-55212877-6